THE OBJECTION OF MY AFFECTION

Written By
CYNTHIA A. KING

Content Warning

This book contains adult content, including themes of narcissistic abuse and explicit language.

To Helen Johnson
A very listener, even if I have to pay her.

TABLE OF CONTENTS

Chapter One

Where did that darn dog go to now? Mary Margaret thought. *I wanted to get her to walk in before it got too hot.* "Stella! Stella!" She called, but her calls were left unanswered. She walked over to the side of the garage where she parked her car to see if Stella had unearthed a treasure and was hiding it for later, but no dog. Mary Margaret went to pick up a ball that rolled to the back of the garage near several empty paint cans left scattered about. Jason, the young guy who mowed her lawn, also painted the back porch but didn't take care of the cans. Mary Margaret wondered if he had hidden those cans to be taken care of later and had forgotten about them, but the word 'later' had no defined end date. She sighed. Jason was a good kid; he'd pick them up when he had a chance.

Why was it so hard for people to follow through these days? Mary Margaret asked herself. *Maybe I should sell the house and buy a condo, I wouldn't need so much help getting things done around here.* It was more house than she needed, now only her and Stella, except this was the place where her daughter Casey grew up. A place of too many firsts. First steps. First solo bike ride. First spring formal dance, pictures taken with her friends in the shade of the big oak tree on the front lawn. She looked at the dent in the wood framing of the garage, the first time Casey took the car out after she got her license. Her old car had a matching dent.

Where is that damn dog anyway? She better not be digging in my rosebushes, Mary Margaret thought as she bent to pick up the ball and straighten the cans when she heard a male voice call out.

✳✳✳

Now that's not something you see every day, John thought to himself as he cooled off from his run in the park. He put his hand up to shield his eyes from the sun. He forgot his sunglasses and the sweat dripped down his face and stung his eyes. It was barely eleven in the morning, and it was already so hot the heat radiated in waves blurring the blacktop.

John squinted his eyes to be sure and watched as the little dog approached him. The dog had the leash clipped to its collar, the other end in its mouth. The dog was walking itself, no owner nearby. He listened to see if someone was calling for it, but the only noise came from the kids on the playground. The dog walked up to him, dropped the leash at his feet, and panted. John immediately snapped out of his daze and scooped the little dog up.

"Hey," he said to the dog as he brought it over to a bench in the shade. "How long have you been walking on the hot tar? Did you burn your little feet?" The dog panted in response. John took what he had left in his water bottle and filled his palm, the dog gratefully lapped it up. "Sorry, sport, that's all I've got. Let's see if your collar can help me get you home."

John turned the collar around and read the tag. It said 'Stella' Greenleaf Terrace, and a phone number. The address was nearby. John decided to bring her home, it wasn't that far out of his way. By the time he got his phone out explained finding the dog, he'd be halfway there. John carried Stella over the shady side of the street and put her down so she could walk home.

John found the house with no trouble; the garage door was up. He could see into the garage; it looked like a normal garage with tools and rakes and a door that opened to the back yard. John saw a pair of garden gloves atop an open bag of potting soil. He opted to try first the front door and pressed the doorbell. John rang it a couple of times, but nobody answered, so he decided to try the garage.

"Hello?" he called out. "Anybody missing a dog?"

"A scruffy a little mutt with a bad attitude? I think she's mine." Mary Margaret yelled back. "I'm in the garage."

John brought the pup into the garage and unclipped the leash. Stella lay down on the cool concrete of the garage floor. He heard a racket coming from the other side of the car parked there. Someone knocked over a bunch of empty paint cans; one rolled harmlessly away into the corner; the rest rolled around in all directions. Amidst the clatter of the cans, he heard a female voice utter a few choice expletives and a woman's head popped up.

"Hello," she said, surprised to see a handsome older man holding her dog's leash in his hand. He looked hot and sweaty, his face red. He was wearing running gear. She was afraid he'd overheat and collapse on her garage floor. "You look like you need a drink. Would you like some water?"

"Do you have a hose?"

"Yes. Over there by the driveway."

She watched him turn the faucet on and soak his head. When he was done, he shook his head like a dog and sprayed droplets everywhere. "Thanks," he said and returned the hose. Before he turned the water off, he sprayed Stella.

"Hey!"

"What? She looked hot, too." He said with a laugh. "Oh, yes, your wayward puppy. She took herself on a long walk so she should sleep good tonight."

John couldn't help but notice how attractive she was. Her hair was medium brown with blonde streaks, either from the sun or a salon. The high humidity caused little tendrils to escape and frame her face. She wore her hair high atop her head in a messy bun, but it only served to accentuate the length of her neck and exposed the tender part of her earlobe. *I could drive her wild making love to that earlobe.* He shook his head to clear the thought.

Mary Margaret's eyes were large and brown; when she smiled, whatever damage time wrought on her face appeared in little crinkles by her eyes, but rather than age her they only added interest to her face.

"She's mine." she said. "Oh, Stella. Couldn't you wait ten minutes? Where did you find her? Sorry about that. If you called, I would have come and picked her up." John didn't think she'd get uglier up close.

"It was the oddest thing. She had her leash in her mouth and was walking herself in the park."

"Stella probably wanted to go before it got too hot. She's smart, sometimes too smart for her own good." Mary Margaret looked down and shook her head at the dog, a slight smile on her lips. "My name is Mary Margaret," she said as she took a step forward to thank him and introduce herself, but instead he heard what sounded like she tripped over a loose can and went down. He heard her say, "FUCK!"

John leaped to her aid. Her head was half under the car, and John was unsure how to help her. Mary Margaret rolled out from underneath; blood covered her face. His eyes opened wide as he looked in alarm at the blood; it ran down her face to her neck, into her ears and soaked her shirt. Stella barked at him and sounded like she was saying, 'Help her! Help her, you moron!'

"Oh, no! What happened? Are you OK?" He reached to help her up and changed his mind. "A towel. You need a towel." John said, his head swiveling around her garage, looking for one.

Mary Margaret pointed in the general direction of a shelf, and he saw the folded pile. John grabbed one and knelt next to her. The blood ran down her face; he wasn't sure from exactly where. He was hesitant about putting on the towel over her brow if she was hurt, and he didn't want to risk hurting her further. Mary Margaret decided for him; she sat up, grabbed the towel and pressed it over her right eye.

"Ow. Ow. Ow." She pulled the towel away and looked at the bloody mess. "How bad is it?"

She watched him blanch at the sight of her.

"Not good. Not good at all. You've got a cut on your eyebrow; it looks pretty deep. You probably need stitches. Keep pressure on it."

"Would you mind putting Stella inside and grabbing the keys? The ones hanging up by the door? I guess I'll go to Urgent Care." Mary Margaret waved towards the door with her free hand.

He did as she asked while Stella whined half-heartedly. The walk must have tired her out; she went to her water bowl, took a long drink, and went to lay down in her bed. He grabbed the keys, said good-bye to Stella, and shut the door. Mary Margaret reached her hand out for her car keys. John pulled them back.

"How are you supposed to drive? You only have one eye. You can't see. Just keep pressure on it. I'll drive." John said and helped her in the car. "Do you need your purse? Your wallet? I.D.?"

"I suppose I need my insurance card. My purse is hanging on a hook by the keys."

He went back inside and grabbed her bag, handed it to her and got in the driver's side. John looked at her before he started the car. It was her misfortune to be wearing a white tank top, more red than white now. It looked like somebody tried to gut her like a fish. The blood hardened in the creases of her neck and in her ears. John drove past the turn that would have brought them to Urgent Care. She pointed it out to him.

"Take you someplace staffed by a moonlighting resident after a 48-hour shift? I don't think so. You're going to the ER and having a plastic surgeon work on you. You're much too pretty for some hack job."

Mary Margaret wanted to give him some wise ass answer like 'who invited you?" and demand her keys back, except he called her pretty, and it had been a while since anybody called her that.

"Thank you. What was your name again? If you told me, I forgot. I was distracted and I don't remember."

"It's John. John Adams. You're Mary Ann? You fell before you said your last name."

"It's Mary Margaret. Welch. It's Mary Margaret Welch." She unfolded the towel, found a clean area and placed it back on her wound.

"How are you feeling, Mary Margaret Welch?"

"Alright, but I'm getting a killer headache. A few things. Thank you for helping me, but I have to warn you."

"Warn me? About what?"

"Me. I'm not a very nice person. I find people exhausting. In fact, I'll push my shopping cart down the closest aisle to avoid talking to somebody. I've been called a bitch more than once, and I usually deserved it. I'm not a warm, fuzzy kind of bitch either. Don't get your feelings hurt if I'm not very nice. Not very nice is my default."

"Thanks for the warning, but I've been called worse."

"I usually do for myself and try to avoid depending on people. I'm nervous you're here, and you're being so nice I feel like there must be some string attached, but my head hurts too much to figure it out."

"Look at it this way: I came along and was lucky enough to be able to lend a helping hand to a stranger. A Good Samaritan, as it were. Straight from the Bible. I'm endorsed by God."

"Wow. I've never met someone endorsed by God before. Thank you. I'll try to be gracious, but I can't promise anything."

John drove around to the ER parking lot. He parked and went to get a wheelchair. Mary Margaret initially refused, but he told her unless she wanted to wait all day, go with it, so she sat down.

"I'm only sitting because I have a wicked headache."

"That doesn't matter. People will think you got stabbed and not mind if you cut ahead of them." John said as he pushed her towards the double doors. There was no line at the Admissions desk. After she filled out her paperwork, he parked her in the waiting room and sat down next to her.

Mary Margaret pulled her phone out and told John her four-digit code, asked him to find Casey in her contacts, and hit send. He handed it back to her as it rang.

"Yeah. It's me. What time's your break? I'm in the ER. Nothing serious. I cut my head. I don't know, some guy. I don't know his name. So what? He doesn't know mine. OK. See you in a few." She hung up and looked at him. "So. What is your name, anyway?"

"I already told you. Who's Casey?"

"My daughter. She's a nurse upstairs."

"Shouldn't you call Mr. Welch and let him know you're here?"

"Mr. Welch. Why would he care?"

"Husbands usually do."

"You're right, except now he's somebody else's husband. We're divorced and have been since Casey was a little kid."

"Oh. Sorry. I didn't mean to pry."

"It's no big deal; it happened so long ago." She shrugged her shoulders with indifference.

"I was wondering if you were single. I'm only in town for the next couple of months and thought someone as charming as yourself must have eligible males lining up outside your door."

"Did you see any?"

"No.

"That's your answer."

"I was wondering what you do for fun, but it doesn't seem you to like to have fun."

"I don't. I'm the crazy cat lady. Don't tell Stella."

"Your secret is safe with me. I won't ruin your reputation as a cantankerous old coot."

Mary Margaret frowned at him. "I wouldn't go that far. Please be quiet. My head is killing me, and it hurts to think."

They sat, not speaking while they waited. Soon, a girl in scrubs and a white lab coat came running around the side closest to the elevators, heading straight for them. Casey pulled up short and looked at her mother's eye. She knelt to examine her, her touch tender and gentle.

"Mom. What did you do now?" She nodded at John. "Who's your friend?"

"I don't know. He won't tell me his name. But he doesn't know mine, so it's OK."

"Quit lying, Mary Margaret. I know where you live. Stella told me." He looked at her daughter. "And you, too, Casey. I was just returning a lost dog and your mother took a header. My name is John Adams, and I happened to be in the right place at the right time to help your charming mother."

"Charming mother?" Casey laughed. "She's been called many things, but charming was never one of them."

"Careful, Casey. You don't want me to be charming all over you. You're not too old to be put up for adoption."

"Don't forget I get to pick your nursing home."

"Are you going to hold that over my head for the rest of my life?"

"How ever short that may be, Mother."

John stayed quiet and watched their exchange. Casey strongly resembled mother, not only in looks but in humor as well. He wondered if Mr. Welch was the kind of guy who'd be annoyed if every time he spoke to his daughter it would be like talking to his ex-wife. He found their exchange enchanting. *Jesus. It's like watching two Kangaroos box. No verbal punches landed, but the exchange was humorous and rapid-fire. Enchanting. Where did that come from?* John thought. *I'm making myself sick. But she is kind of cute, and I imagine when she was blood-free she might be considered beautiful.*

Mary Margaret gave him the once over. John came directly from his run and hadn't changed out of his running clothes. He wore typical running gear, short nylon shorts, and a sleeveless jersey. His hair was already dry. It looked like he took running seriously. Mary Margaret didn't bother to check out his feet; she knew he probably wore expensive running sneakers or shoes. She had no idea what they were called. The only time Mary Margaret ever ran was after Stella when she got loose.

"Don't you need to go home and take a shower? Put some clothes on? I'm surprised you're not cold; this air conditioning is freezing. You can take my car. I'll be here a while." Mary Margaret said.

"You can't let a stranger take your car," Casey said.

"It's a piece of shit. If he wanted to steal a car, it wouldn't be that one. The Lamborghini is in the shop."

He noticed her looking at him, her expression unreadable.

"Are my clothes making you uncomfortable?" He said with a smirk.

"No. Your *lack* of clothes is making me uncomfortable." She smirked back.

"Here." John said. "Give me your phone." She handed him her phone. Mary Margaret was curious why he wanted it. He unlocked it, put his name and number in her contacts, and gave it back. John stood up and dangled her keys.

"I'll go home and take a shower. I'll even change my clothes. I should be back soon. If you need me for anything, my number's in there." He turned, walked out the exit, and left.

Casey grabbed the phone. "Give that to me." She looked at the blank screen. "What's your code? Wait a minute. How come he knows your code, and I don't? You won't even tell me."

"I gave it to him so I could call you. I must not be thinking straight. Maybe I have a concussion from when I hit my head." Casey snapped into her medical mode and grabbed a penlight from her pocket. She reached towards her mother's face.

"Here. Let me look at your eye." She shone the light into her mother's face. Mary Margaret pushed her hand away.

"I'm fine. I hit my head on a metal shelf. I didn't lose consciousness."

"You are definitely not fine. You gave some guy your access code. He's driving your car. He can get in your garage and rob the place. Some guy you don't even know his name, for goodness' sake. He could be lying about his name."

9

"I know how to find out. The number's 1013. Look under contacts." Casey followed her mother's direction and searched for his entry. She smiled. October thirteenth was her birthday.

"Shoot. He just put in the name John. It's probably fake. I need to go now. Bye, Mom. Call me if something new happens; otherwise, call me when you get home." She ran off in the direction of the elevator. Mary Margaret heard her call out, 'hold the elevator, please.' She smiled to herself; at least her daughter remembered her manners.

Mary Margaret sat there and waited, for her name to be called, for John to come back with her car, for people to stop staring at the bloody mess that covered her. Mary Margaret took the towel off her eye, turned it around, and looked for an unsaturated area to put back on her injury. She hoped she was called next because she was running out of clean towel. *Yeah, what is wrong with me, giving a total stranger the keys to my house? He is kind of cute, and in pretty good shape judging by his running clothes,* she thought. *Thinking like that about a stranger, about him or any other guy, but he is good-looking. Eww. Has it really been that long since she was interested in a man? Remotely interested? That conk on the head must have really knocked me for a loop.*

Mary Margaret looked around the waiting room at her competition. Triage, Casey called it. One guy came in on a stretcher, and she figured he'd move up ahead of her. A young couple came in; they were looking for someone who'd already been brought back to the exam rooms. Her headache felt better if she closed both eyes; otherwise, it made her dizzy. She leaned back and tried to get comfortable but couldn't. Mary Margaret's eyes were closed when John returned.

"Hey, sleeping beauty. Wake up."

She opened her eye and squinted at him in the harsh fluorescent light. He was wearing regular clothes, khaki shorts and a striped golf shirt. "Wake up? I wish. I'm stuck in this nightmare thinking this is the ER and it's really the DMV. Would you please check at the desk and see how much longer? It feels like I've been here forever."

"No."

"No? NO? I said 'please,' that's more than most people get. Look, I don't know you. You're really getting on my last nerve. To be honest, I don't know if I even like you. Give me my keys and go. There's no reason for you to stay. I know you probably feel guilty because you're the reason I fell in the first place, but I forgive you." She took a twenty out of her purse and handed it to him. "Call an Uber. You were very kind to help me, but you can go now."

"No. We're waiting for someone. By the way, we're here because you're a klutz, and you tripped. I'm not responsible for that. I didn't push you." John pointed out, with a slight smile. "Blame Stella. She's the reason I was at your house in the first place." He put the money in his pocket.

"That damn dog. She probably brought you home on purpose to piss me off."

"Does she usually pick up guys in the park?"

"No. You're the first."

"I'm flattered."

"Don't be. She once brought home a dead squirrel."

***

Mary Margaret had a chance to look at him in regular clothes. He was right, his running clothes did make her uncomfortable. The lack of fabric meant he was exposing a lot of flesh, his uncovered limbs and armpits. She had a personal bias regarding men and their armpits. She didn't like seeing them. Mary Margaret decided she'd give him a pass because he was on his way home from running.

She tried to look at him without being obvious but giving him the side eye was out since he was sitting next to her, and it made her nauseous. Mary Margaret turned her head towards him under the pretense of changing the towel to a dry spot, but there was very little left. She turned it this way and that; tried to sneak a look at him.

His face looked nice and pleasant, without evil or guile. John had clear blue eyes with the ubiquitous creases that come with aging, as well as the deep lines bracketing his smile. He had an aquiline nose judging from his profile. True, his hair was thinning and gray, but he still had enough left for him not to be obsessed with it. Mary Margaret had to admit he was handsome.

He changed into a pair of khaki chino shorts and a blue and white striped polo shirt. He looked starched and pressed; she looked like the contents of an evidence bag. After a while a short, balding man approached them, wearing the ugly plaid pants golfer's favor. John stood up and greeted him.

"Mark. Thanks for coming. Mary Margaret, I'd like to introduce you to Dr. Mark Stewart, plastic surgeon." She was happy to see him. It looked like she'd soon be taken care of and able to leave.

"Dr. Stewart, thanks for coming. I'm not sure why I deserve special treatment, but I'll take it." She removed the towel so he could see what brought him in on what looked like a day off. He leaned over, looked at her injury, and nodded.

"Yes, this will definitely require stitches. I'll get someone to bring you back while I change into some scrubs." He walked to the desk, spoke to a nurse and headed off to change. A nurse came and took her wheelchair into an exam room.

"I'm not sure who you know to have the head of Plastics make a special trip here during the weekend but consider yourself lucky. He's the best," the nurse said. "You won't even have a scar. Hop up on this stretcher, and he'll be right in." She got on the table, the nurse took the wheelchair and left. Mary Margaret was surprised to see John leaning against the wall. He followed them in.

"John, I'm grateful for your help, I really am, but you've done enough. I'm sure you're not allowed in here. I've got a bad headache and I'm in a miserable mood. I'm usually not good company even if I don't hit my head. See, if you're nice to me, I feel obligated to be nice back, and with a headache like this I can't be nice. It takes a lot out of me, being nice. So go."

"You already told me about your misanthropic tendencies so don't worry about it." John looked at her. "You don't need to be nice, you need to relax. I promise not to tease you anymore. I was trying to distract you from your injury, that's all."

"So, you didn't come in to see me cry? How did you get the big gun to interrupt his day off for a stupid little cut? You shouldn't have wasted a favor on me."

"My mistake. Are you going to cry? At least then, it wouldn't be a total waste. Please don't tough it out on my account. Feel free to cry your eye out." He laughed at his joke. "Sorry."

Before Mary Margaret could respond, the nurse came in with the needed supplies, opened a couple of suture packs and set it all up for the doctor. He walked in dressed in scrubs, thanked the nurse for her help, and put on some gloves. The doctor came to the head of the bed and looked down at her. John got up and stood opposite him.

"Pardon me; I'm Doctor Mark Stewart. If John mentioned your name, I didn't catch it."

"You can call her a miserable old bat. I saw it on her insurance card when she checked in." John answered for her. She got up on her elbows and tried to get off the table, ready to strangle him. "I'm not a miserable old bat. I'm a miserable *young* bat. Besides, isn't it illegal or something if he's in here? He's violating my rights."

"She does have a point. Only relatives allowed with the patient's permission, John."

"Relax. I'm just trying to lighten the mood. Her name is Mary Margaret Something or other. She's in pain and I'm making it worse. I think she broke her sense of humor, her humerus." He laughed again. "Sorry. I'll stop now. My apologies."

"John, you're not funny. Stop laughing at your own stupid jokes, nobody else thinks you're funny. Doctor, tell him to shut up. He's yanking my chain on purpose."

"John, please stop harassing my patient. I will toss you out of here if the patient requests. Mary Margaret. You want him gone?" The doctor asked. "I had a fifth-grade teacher named Sister Mary Margaret. Now, she was a miserable old bat. You didn't use to be a nun, did you?"

"Not the way she curses," John said.

"You," she said to John. "Who let you in here anyway? Say one more word, and I'll have him sew your mouth shut. Doctor, can we get started, please?"

John figured he better shut up or he will end up in the waiting room. "Not another word," he promised. He also noticed she didn't request security haul him out, so he really should shut up.

"You bet. I'm going to have to numb the area. I'm not going to lie; it's going to hurt. I could say you might feel a little sting, but you seem too smart to fall for that." He swabbed her brow with Betadine, took the syringe, and said, "I'll try to go as quickly as I can if you try not to move."

Mary Margaret wouldn't give John the satisfaction of seeing her weak, she wasn't in the habit of letting anyone see her weak. She stayed perfectly still as much as she wanted to scream. Soon the lidocaine started to work. Mary Margaret lay there quietly while he worked. He talked to John while he sewed. From the conversation, she gathered they golfed together. She wished John would shut up; he was distracting the doctor.

Mary Margaret watched the doctor sew her up. His hands worked quick and sure, disengaged from his mouth. He could talk as much as he wanted, but his hands were operating independently of his voice. The overhead light shined bright in her eyes, so she closed them. Other than a slight tug here and there, she felt very little. She heard the tray clatter as he put the instruments down; the nurse appeared to help clean her up.

"John said you fell and hit your head on a metal shelf. It wasn't a nice clean cut like something sharp; it was a bit difficult without smooth edges, but I think overall, you'll be pleased with the result once it heals. You may have a black eye and a bit of a knot, but it wasn't as bad as it looked. The head bleeds a lot when injured. Cathy will help clean you up. I'll leave the follow-up notes upfront. Mary Margaret, it was a pleasure. John, step outside and give her some room."

The men left the room; the nurse Cathy came over with a wet towel and cleaned her up as best she could. She needed a tetanus shot, something Mary Margaret didn't remember agreeing to and not very pleased about getting but did so without complaint. When she finished, Cathy brought the wheelchair back, seated Mary Margaret, and exited the room. John waited for her in the hall, he already picked up her paperwork. He tried to get the wheelchair away from Cathy, but she told him the hospital policy was for him to pull the car upfront and Cathy would help her into the vehicle. Once accomplished, Mary Margaret thanked Cathy profusely for her soft touch and tender care. John pulled out and headed back to her house.

"That took up almost the whole afternoon, and you didn't eat lunch. Would you like me to get something for you before you go home? At least when you're ready to eat, you'll have something already prepared."

"You have a point. I didn't eat lunch or breakfast either."

"No wonder you fell. You probably got dizzy because you're hypoglycemic."

"On a first-name basis with the head of plastic surgery? Using words like 'hypoglycemic'? Who are you, John? Is that even your first name?"

"Busted. I usually go by John Doe. My ex-wife liked to think I was John Dough the way she spent money. I know Mark because he did my wife's first boob job. I know what hypoglycemic means since I suffer from it." He looked at her to see if she bought any of it. Her face remained unmoved by his explanation. "OK, I know Mark from golf, and he did do my ex-wife's boob job, but that was years ago. He was my roommate in college. I know what hypoglycemia is because I'm not an idiot. Now it's gluten. Or lactose."

"That's good enough for me." Mary Margaret said. "I probably should get something to eat. There's not much to eat at my house. If you don't mind taking me to get a sandwich, I can eat it whenever."

He pulled into the SubStop Shop on the corner and asked for her order. She reached into her bag, but he was out of the car before she had a chance to hand him some money. John came back shortly with two sandwiches, and handed her the change from the twenty she gave him earlier. She looked at them, and he said, "I missed lunch, too." He drove her home and helped her inside. John sat her at the kitchen table and looked inside her fridge. "Beer, soda, or water?"

"I'll have a bottle of water, thanks. Help yourself to whatever you'd like. Are you planning on staying?"

"Yes, if you don't mind. As I said, I didn't eat lunch either. After we eat and I get you settled, I'll take off. Would you like me to walk Stella, too?"

Mary Margaret looked at him and wondered what angle he was working. *What's he got to gain from any of this?* She thought. *Are there still men who don't have a hidden agenda? He must feel sorry for me, a lonely, divorced, post menopausal woman with only a dog for company.*

It made her headache worse to think about it, so she stopped. She ate half her sandwich and wrapped up the leftovers for later.

"You didn't finish your sandwich. Are you feeling nauseous?" John asked, concerned about her.

"No, I'm feeling full. I'll eat the rest of it for dinner. You don't have to hang around. I'm good."

John stood up and cleared the table. He even took a wet paper towel and wiped it down. He put her sandwich in the fridge and asked where the recyclables went. His competency around a kitchen impressed her. Her ex-husband never picked up after her. Or himself.

"Now, where would you like to go? Do you want to lay on the couch, or go to bed?"

"Since it's still light outside, I think it's a no-go for bed. I'll just lay on the couch." When she stood up, Stella got up too. She started to wiggle her hind end excitedly. She had a nice nap while Mary Margaret was at the hospital and was ready to go. Stella jumped up and down in anticipation of her afternoon walk. "Not now, Stella. I need to rest a little." She jumped up on the couch to tell Mary Margaret she wanted her walk. "No, Stella. Not now. I have to lay down."

John approached with Stella's leash. "I'll take her, so she won't bother you later. You lay there and relax." He clipped Stella's leash and handed her the remote. "We'll take an extra-long one. I'll get her good and tired."

"You know you have to pick up her poop. There are bags in that canister attached to her leash."

"If I wanted to pick up poop I'd have my own dog," he agreed reluctantly. "What do I do after I pick it up?"

"Carry it until you find a garbage can. You may have to bring it back here."

"I'll take her to the park. There are cans there. I'll pick it up, but I'm not carrying it around." John took Stella for a nice long walk in the park, so she didn't bother Mary Margaret later. Stella was very kind to him. She pooped next to a garbage can. He had less than a yard to handle it. "Good girl, Stella. Thank you for this."

John took her for another lap around the park and brought her home. He let them in and she stood near her water dish. He filled it, she drank her fill, and left to find Mary Margaret. He hung up her leash and followed her to the couch, Stella whined to get her attention.

"Not now, Stella. She's sleeping."

Mary Margaret reached out her hand and scratched the little dog's neck. "I'm not sleeping. I feel OK. My head only aches when I move around. Come on, Stella. Up. Squeeze in here." The little dog jumped up and squished herself between Mary Margaret and the couch cushions until just her head poked out. She rested her head on her owner's hip and looked at John.

"Well, would you like me to do anything else? Stella had a nice long walk so she shouldn't bother you later. Where do you keep your Tylenol? I'll get you some before I go."

She pointed at the cupboard over the sink.

He brought her two, left two for later and gave her a bottle of water. "Is there anything else you need? If not, I'll take off now."

She thought *move in here and take care of us until we die.* Instead, she said, "I think you've done more than enough. Thank you very much, John. You've been more than kind, but you can go now." *There. Casey will be so proud I behaved like a normal, rational human being.*

"Mary Margaret, it was my pleasure. I was glad to help." He walked to the door, opened it and looked back at her. "You're not that bad, you know."

"What does that mean?"

"Your bark is worse than your bite."

"If I felt better, you'd feel my bite."

"You have a very pretty smile. I'd hate for you to chip a tooth on my heart of stone."

"What does that mean? You don't have a heart of stone. I never said that."

"Contrary to popular belief you don't either. Goodbye, Mary Margaret." He left and shut the door behind him.

"Ugh." She and Stella shut their eyes and fell fast asleep.

When she woke, it was five o'clock in the morning and she was ravenous, so she ate the other half of her sandwich. Mary Margaret took a shower to wash away the residual blood and put on clean sweats. She let Stella out to do her business. They went back to the couch, and she fell asleep with no trouble at all.

Chapter Two

Mary Margaret woke later that morning; she felt almost human. She looked at her face in the bathroom mirror. Her eye was swollen and turning a lovely shade of purple. She was barely able to keep it open. The doctor's handiwork evidence of his excellent reputation; the cut was barely visible. It just looked like she went a few rounds with Mike Tyson. Her hair, however, was a different problem. She slept on it wet, and it dried haphazardly. Part of it looked regular, parts of it stuck up. Mary Margaret sighed, turned off the bathroom light, and went to make coffee. The doorbell rang while she filled up the carafe with water. She went over to unlock the door. As she pulled it open, Mary Margaret saw John and waved him in. He came in with coffee and donuts.

"Here. I brought you some coffee. I wanted to see how you made out."

"I made out just fine. Is this like when a fighter asks his trainer to cut him? To stop the swelling so he can see?"

"I've never boxed, so I can't say. Were you ever a boxer?" He asked her.

"Obviously not, or I wouldn't have asked you. I was thinking about the movie Rocky when he asked Burgess Meredith to cut him. Because that's pretty much what happened, only I cut it before. The blood didn't have a chance to pool up because it bled all over me."

"Sounds plausible. Here. Drink your coffee before it gets cold. There's sugar and creamer in the bag. I wasn't sure how you take it. I brought you some donuts, though. It was a big risk. You might be one of those women who hasn't had a carb since college." He changed the subject. "I'm glad to see you're up and about. You might want to do something with your hair, though, if you plan on leaving the house."

"Yeah." She said as she sipped her coffee. She looked into the box that contained the donuts and looked back at him, a puzzled look on her face. "You know I, like

19

most women, have a love/hate relationship with carbs, like bagels. I'll eat them, but only one particular kind. Same with donuts. There is only one kind I'll eat. For taking a shot in the dark, you did well." She pulled a glazed chocolate donut out. "This one."

"You can't have that one. That one's mine. Pick another." She broke the donut in half and handed him a chunk.

"Thank you," he said. John took a bite with a sip of his coffee. "Tell me, do you have a nickname? Mary Margaret's quite a mouthful."

"Too many. Mostly it's like this: MaryM, or Mary Em. It goes back to first grade. There was another Mary. She was Mary C. I've been called that for most of my life, 'Mary M.' Mary C. moved away in third grade, but I was still Mary M. It never changed. So, it's Marym. I embraced it the best I could. It's like Miriam. Maryem. That's stuck with me all my life. Oh, yeah. Like my last name, Miller. Two Ms. Mary Margaret, Eminem. Taken. Mary Margaret Miller, 3M. Taken. So Marym it is unless you can come up with something better. Tell me, John, what's your name? Is there a story that dresses it up? John is pretty white bread."

"What if I told you my last name is Adams and my ancestors came over on the Mayflower?"

"I'd say you're full of shit."

"Well, you'd be wrong." He pulled out his wallet and handed her a business card. It read 'John Q. Adams, Adams Information Management and Computer Analyst. "The Q stands for Quincy."

"I guess I would be," she said as she turned the card over in her hand. "You have quite the pedigree. I'm sorry to tell you my ancestors are sketchier and far more nefarious. I'm a gutter rat compared to you."

"I don't mind slumming," he said, looking her in the eye. "Not a bit. Your daughter, Casey, is she an only child?"

"Yes. We weren't together long enough to give her a sibling. It was one of those marrying your best friend deal. We got married after college because we never found anybody else we liked as much as each other. We never argued or had any fights, no throwing of dishes or vases. We never even raised our voices. It was exactly what you'd want in a partner, except passion. It's hard to get excited over an old, comfortable shoe." Mary Margaret winced, from either the pain from her eye or the memory. John wanted to ask which, but he knew better than to interrupt her if he wanted to hear the rest of the story.

"Ben, my ex-husband, discovered that after a chance meeting with a woman on an elevator. He said he was sorry, but he had no idea what it meant to fall in love until it happened to him. After they got off the elevator, Ben invited her for a drink. My husband called me the next morning; he couldn't wait to tell me he found someone who thrilled him to the bone. He said he wanted that for me, too. Ben told me I deserved it and shouldn't settle for anything less; this might be a bad way to go about it, but we needed to divorce. Not 'I want a divorce; we *need* to divorce.' It worked out well for him; her name is Sheila. They married, had a few more kids. They live locally, and we all raised Casey."

"What about you? How'd you feel about it?"

"Me? I felt embarrassed. Not really hurt, well yeah, I hurt for a while. What he said made sense. As far as the grand passion needed to sustain a relationship, when he was with her, he was a completely different guy. I could see what depth he had with her he never had with me. Ben being right didn't help much in the beginning. Like I said, I felt embarrassed. Stupid, even. How did I miss signs that were so obvious looking back?

"I was busy with a baby and a job and never questioned if there was supposed to be more. That was a long time ago. In the end we stayed friends; I love Sheila like a sister. Their kids are like my nieces and nephews. Casey is as much a part of their family as her half-siblings. It's a mutually sustainable dynamic. I'm sure most people would think our having so civil a divorce to the point where we spend holidays together might seem odd, but it works for us. We all know our roles, and everybody respects everyone else, so it's cool. Beats eating toast by yourself on Christmas morning. We are all related some how by marriage or birthdays or in-laws and so much is ancient history. The old ones with the grudges have all died off, but people like to cause drama. They say things back and forth. I don't care, let somebody else keep track.

"That's more than you need to know about me. What's your story? You can't offer up the 'we made better friends than lovers' excuse. You bought your wife new boobs, so there must have been a little heat there. There had to be. Why bother making the investment if you weren't going to be around to enjoy them?"

"Yes, why? Maybe it was like pissing down well. I'd thrown everything else at her trying to make her happy, why not new tits? I have two sons. Once they were established as self-sufficient adults and gone, I think she viewed me as the comfortable old shoe. She wanted to shed the mother label for the Babe one, but that's not how life works, is it? She underwent a complete overhaul on the outside; it's too bad she didn't bother investing in herself internally.

"True, the tennis pro didn't seem to mind. Neither did the neighbor. She left for greener pastures. Or maybe one that wasn't going gray. About five years ago, she moved down south, following an affair with some corporate honcho. She moved all that way only to end up as a side piece; the other woman, as it were. She wasn't going to be hosting some holiday extravaganza; she wasn't even invited. His wife knew all about her. The family roasting chestnuts by a roaring fire did not include her. She now lives near my youngest, Peter, outside Dallas. Any financial obligation I had towards her is long over.

"My move here is predicated on a long-term IT project with the University. Dr. Stewart, the guy that fixed your face was my college roommate. He moved here to take a position with the medical school, so there was that. Here is nice. No bad memories. No negative energy. I haven't been here long enough to be exposed to its steamy underbelly, unless you're interested in showing me yours."

Mary Margaret looked at him. That was the oddest pickup line ever heard. She opened her mouth to answer when she heard the cranking gears of the garage door going up. Casey entered through the door leading into the kitchen.

"Oh, hey, Mom. I've come to look at your eye. Who's car-" she stopped when she saw John. "Still hanging around her? She hasn't pulled out her .45 and scared you away?"

John shook his head no.

22

"Don't worry. She will. Just try not to take it personal when she does." Casey told him. "Have you been here all this time?"

"No. I just got here and brought coffee and donuts." He passed her the box. "Donut?"

"Thanks," Casey said. "If not now, when?" She held up a donut. Casey turned back to her mother, licking the frosting as it melted around her fingertips. She chose the donut known as the Bismark. Cream filling topped with chocolate icing. *Good choice*, he thought. *My other favorite.* He knew it was dumb, but he thought about it, how they had similar tastes, and he smiled. *Like they were related, almost.*

While Mary Margaret talked with her daughter, John was able to take a good look at her. He met her for the first time yesterday under less-than-ideal circumstances. Now John observed her with her guard down and not distracted by blood or Betadine. He guessed her age to be over fifty based on her having an adult child.

Her hair was still messed up from sleeping on it wet, but it was a pretty brown color with lighter streaks throughout; it fell just below her shoulders. She had uncommonly light brown eyes, or eye, with little flecks of green and dark eyelashes. She had a nice smile with straight white teeth. Casey looked like a lot her mother, only younger. He thought Casey was very attractive. Even though she was older, had a black eye and a lump on her brow, he thought time had been kind to Mary Margaret.

"What are you looking at?" She caught him staring at her and didn't sound pleased about it.

"Your eye," he told her. "I'm not looking at you. I'm watching Casey evaluate your eye." *Nice recovery*, he thought.

Casey looked at her mother's injury. "Damn. That's perfect. How you got Dr. Stewart to come in on a Saturday nobody can explain. He just comes in off the golf course to sew up a stranger's head, then he leaves to finish his round. I underestimate you, Mother. You have friends in high places."

"I wish I could take credit, but it was all him. Dr. Stewart's a very good friend of his and did him the favor. He's the one with connections, Casey, not me."

"You're connected to him. Another degree of separation, but still." She looked at John indirectly. *The first guy who made inroads with mother. He seemed nice enough,* she thought. Her Mother's reaction surprised her. She's seen her bare enough teeth to frighten away any guy who expressed interest, but this guy didn't seem scared of her in the least.

Maybe that conk on the head knocked some sense into her mother, like in the movies. Somebody gets hit on the head and undergoes a personality change. Her mom wasn't necessarily bitter and vindictive, she was more like indifferent to men and relationships, best left to hopeless romantics. But this guy, John, totally missed the 'proceed with caution' sign her mother threw up. Or maybe he didn't care. Here he sat with Marym two days in a row without a wound to show for it. *Huh,* thought Casey.

"I've got to go, Mom. I'm working nights in the ER this week. I wanted to see if you needed anything, but you look like you'll survive without me," she said as she finished the donut and licked her fingers. She got up and kissed her mother on the cheek. "Good-bye, John. If I never see you again, thanks for all your help." She exited the way the way she came in and was gone.

"What does she mean, 'if I never see you again?'"

"I think she means I'm very self-sufficient. There's no reason for you to stop by again."

He looked her in the eye again. "I can think of a million reasons. Right now, I think I'll take Stella out for a walk. Would you like to go for a walk, Stella?" Stella came out from under the table where she waited for scraps. She went over to the hook that held her leash, grabbed it in her mouth and pulled it down. She walked back to John, dropped the leash at his feet and sat. She waited patiently for him to clip it to her collar. John looked at Marym. "That's quite a trick."

"Yes. Yes, it is. I wish I could say I taught her that, but she figured it out on her own."

"Is there any way to teach her to pick up her poop?"

She shook her head no and laughed while he attached the leash. "If there were, she'd never let on she knew. That's the human's job."

John took Stella for a nice walk through the park. He couldn't believe a little dog could draw such a crowd of pretty girls. He had to stop a couple of times to let the girls oh and ah over Stella. If John were younger, having a dog would automatically increase his pool of dating prospects. As it was, he wasn't interested in these young girls in short shorts and tiny tank tops. He kind of liked Mary Margaret. She had some history to her. He didn't know why he was interested, but he was. He wanted to see what lay behind her façade.

John brought Stella back. She drank half her water dish and headed to her bed. Her tail thumped against the floor in an acknowledgment of Mary Margaret. She looked at the little dog crashed out on her bed.

"She has to be exhausted; you were gone quite a while."

"We had to stop and say hello a number of times. She's a very popular girl."

"Well, thank you very much for the coffee and donuts, and Stella thanks you for her walk."

"You're both very welcome," John said. He didn't sit down or leave. He leaned against the wall and stood silently.

"What? Why are you still here?"

"I want to ask you something, but I'm not sure how to go about it."

"Let me save you the trouble. Whatever it is, the answer is 'no.'"

"How can you give a blanket 'no' when you don't know what I wanted to ask?"

"Let's see. I bet it involves fixing my hair. You're a real nice guy, John. You are. I consider myself socially awkward. I'm not good at small talk, or any kind of talk, honestly. I usually piss most people off. I can hear Casey saying 'you shouldn't be so rude, Mom. He's been nothing but nice. Plaster a smile on your face and be nice back.' That would mean I'm being fake. It's a toss-up. Which would you prefer? Rude or Fake?"

John remained silent and looked at her, his face unreadable. He held her gaze a minute. "I know we met in less-than-ideal circumstances, Marym, but I thought hidden under your push-the-world-away exterior might beat the heart of a nice woman, but I guess I was wrong. Goodbye, Stella." He said, turned around and headed for the door. "No need to show me to the door. I know where it is." He walked out and shut the door behind him.

Mary Margaret watched him leave. She knew what he wanted, he wanted to ask her out. Sooner or later it always came down to it. She took the offensive and shut it down before he became more curious about her. Years ago, she took herself out of the dating pool. A very scary relationship scarred her and left her with the inability to trust her own instincts, unable to commit. She decided something must be wrong with her to attract such guys. Mary Margaret no longer trusted herself. He seemed like a nice enough guy. There was no sense in leading him on.

It made no sense, but ever since her marriage imploded, she didn't trust her own judgement. Even though it's been years, somewhere deep down it still hurt as much as it ever did. *They say you should marry your best friend if you want to be happy,* she thought. *Boy, did I call that wrong.* It wasn't that she didn't trust John; she didn't trust herself. Her few other attempts at love didn't end well either.

Chapter Three

John stirred up her insides, forcing things Mary Margaret couldn't reconcile to rise to the surface and demand her attention. It wasn't true she never tried to get back out there and find the grand passion Ben told her she deserved. She dated a bit, but no man who would cause her to divorce her spouse and run away with him crossed her path. When Casey was in third grade she met Mike at a PTA meeting. He asked her to go for coffee afterward. She said yes. Mary Margaret liked him immediately. Mike seemed like a genuinely good guy. He fell into the tall, dark, and handsome category. He was the father of three boys, one in kindergarten and younger twins. Mike had been separated almost a year.

Mary Margaret figured he'd had enough time and distance so the topic of his wife wouldn't dominate the conversation; for the most part, she didn't. He did ask a lot of questions about divorce, being divorced, getting a divorce, parenting children of divorce. Mike rented a house right around the corner from his former home. They worked out an arrangement where he had his boys Monday through Sunday, he would drop them off Sunday night and his wife had them the following Monday through Sunday. He had blocks of free time they would spend together, hiking or exploring places like antique shops. They went to the farmers market and music festivals.

They had a lot of fun together; both felt it was too early to involve the children. Mary Margaret was blindsided when at dinner one night he told her was getting back together with his wife and couldn't see her anymore. She said "oh" and reached for her purse. Mary Margaret took a couple of twenties out and put them down on the table and stood up.

"That should cover it. I'm going outside and calling a ride. Please don't follow me. Good luck with your wife. If it doesn't work out don't call me." She said and ran out the door marked Exit. Mary Margaret didn't want to cry in the backseat of some stranger's car so she started walking most of the way home. She did end up calling Ben from a gas station pay phone because the restaurant was on the other side of town; by then she was all cried out and her feet were killing her. Sheila came and picked her up. Mary Margaret blamed herself for being so stupid.

***

It was a few years later when she met Dan. She was at the drug store when Dan approached her. He was incredibly charming and very good looking. He walked her to her car and asked her to lunch. There was a cafe in the same plaza; Mary Margaret was hungry, so she said yes. She had no intention of it going any further than lunch. She even paid for her own.

Dan was funny. He poked and prodded Mary Margaret until she told him way more than she wanted to reveal. He focused on her like a laser. His attention and flattery made her feel special. He got her to give up her phone number and called her a few hours later. They must have spent over an hour on the phone, talking mostly about Mary Margaret. He asked her to dinner the next day and she said yes. He wanted to pick her up at her house and she gave him her address. Casey was at Ben's and wouldn't be around, so there was no reason not to. He came on like wildfire, almost consuming her.

He brought her flowers. The next three months were just a blur. He managed to get her in bed by the end of the first month. Maybe this was the grand passion Ben talked about. It certainly was intense. Either she was with him or Casey. He left no room for anybody else. Ben worried about it, something about Dan made him uneasy. One day after he dropped Casey off, he asked Mary Margaret to walk him out.

"Hey, I know this isn't any of my business, but don't you think things with Dan are moving a bit too fast? You haven't had a minute to yourself. Even when you're home, you're on the phone. Casey said you hardly talk to her anymore. I think his behavior is excessive. He should back off and give you some room to breathe." Mary Margaret started to say something, but Ben cut her off. "I don't want to talk about it. I just want you to think about. Like I said, it's none of my business."

She went in the house and looked at her daughter. Ben was right. She was so caught up with Dan Mary Margaret wasn't giving Casey her full attention. Maybe Ben was on to something; she did need some room. She thought about Dan, and it was true. He never left her any space to move; he barely ever left her time to think. He dominated her, and Mary Margaret felt crushed under his will. The phone rang. It was Dan. It was almost like he could sense her doubt, and he had to squash it before it took hold.

Mary Margaret felt the hair on the back of her neck rise. He wanted to talk but she told him she was busy with Casey. He wanted to stop by and meet Casey. Mary Margaret told him it was too early to involve her, and he'd meet her soon enough. She told him there was school function and they were on the way out.

"Call me when you get home." Dan told her. It wasn't a request. It was an order.

Mary Margaret suddenly got spooked and said, "Come on, Casey. Let's go get dinner. You pick where we go."

"Yay!" Said Casey. "I want to go to Tony's!"

"In the mood for Italian? Works for me. Let me grab my bag, and let's go."

Mary Margaret was glad she chose a full-service sit-down restaurant. Her phone rang, she could hear it in her purse. She pulled it out and saw it was Dan. Ben was right, he was impacting her relationship with her daughter. Casey was in sixth grade, and soon her friends would replace Mary Margaret as far as with whom she'd want to spend her free time. She was in complete denial about Dan and his need for total control, for his need to negate anything she thought of as less than. His need for control gradually spilled over into other areas of her life until he totally dominated her.

Time with her daughter became precious. It was priceless, soon she'd go off with her friends and college. It was time she wouldn't get back, and decided it was over with Dan Bauer. He had no place in her life and was wasting time with him she'd never get back. Casey wouldn't be little much longer, and Mary Margaret thought she wanted to be with Casey any chance she had. Dan Bauer had to go. She turned the phone off and shoved it deep in her bag. After dinner they went home, cuddled on the couch and watched TV until it was time for bed. Casey went up to her room to read before she went to sleep. Mary Margaret was straightening up when she heard someone pounding on her front door. She looked out and saw Dan. She opened the door, and before he had a chance to push his way in, she stepped out, closing the door behind her. As soon as she was outside Dan started yelling at her.

"Where have you been? I've been calling and you didn't answer. I don't like not being able to get ahold of you."

"I told you I was busy. It was a music recital, and I turned my phone off. I forgot to turn it back on. Geez, relax. Keep your voice down. Casey's inside."

"Don't tell me to be quiet." He yelled. He got right up in her face. "I want you to keep you phone on all the time in case I want to talk to you. I need to know where you are at all times."

Mary Margaret put her hands on his chest to push him back. It was her turn to yell. "Back up! You're crowding me."

He grabbed her wrists and squeezed them, hard. "Don't you ever tell me what to do. Ever." He squeezed her wrists harder and pressed against her, pinning her hands against her chest. "You got that, Mary Margaret? You better watch yourself."

"Things okay over there, Mary Margaret?" It was her neighbor, Mr. Watson, who came out on his porch to see the source of the noise.

"Everything's fine, Mr. Watson. He was just leaving." Under her breath, she said, "Get off me, NOW. Get out of here or I'll have him call the cops." He backed up and let go of her wrists.

"Remember what I said. Keep your phone on." He said as he walked away. She quickly went inside and locked the door. She looked at her wrists. They were red from his grip. She made sure the doors were shut and locked; the alarm turned on. She looked out the front window and made sure he was gone.

***

She was working at the University in the Art Department. She was lucky she had a job in her field, her college major was in Fine Arts. What she was doing had nothing to do with the Fine Arts. She was doing inventory in Ceramics at the time.

Parking was an issue on campus; there wasn't any. She didn't mind taking the shuttle to the off-campus parking lot. The Dean probably had to park there parking was that dear on the hill.

The day after Dan showed up on her front steps, he called her phone five times. Each time she texted him 'working w/boss. Can't talk.' She called him on her lunch hour. "Look, Dan, I'm at work. The policy is no personal calls. I'm sorry but I can't talk."

"Use the restroom. You need to return my calls."

"OK, Dan. I'll try." She decided not to antagonize him. Dan was starting to scare her. Mary Margaret wanted to slow things down, but he responded by being more controlling. When she brought it up, he became angry and more aggressive, and he would verbally beat her down she practically agreed to anything so that he would stop.

Later that afternoon she took the shuttle and got off at her stop. She walked to her car and stopped dead in her tracks. Dan was leaning against her car with a bouquet of flowers. She felt goosebumps rise on her skin and tasted fear in the back of her throat.

"Dan. What are you doing? How did you get past the guard?" He made her very nervous, showing up at her work like that. *Was there nowhere out of his reach?* Mary Margaret thought.

"What's the matter? Aren't you happy to see me?" He wasn't smiling. His eyes looked hard, daring her to challenge him.

"Surprised, that's all. Usually the guard checks for a parking permit."

"I showed him the flowers and said I wanted to surprise my girlfriend. Come here and give me a kiss, girlfriend." She figured just a peck on the lips, but that wasn't what he had in mind. He held her fast against the car and started making out with her to show her who's in charge. She felt like he was trying to lay claim to her and show everyone that she belonged to him. "Let's go back to your place for a quickie. I've been dreaming about it all day."

"I'm not sure we'll have time. I have to pick up Casey from school."

Dan knew that Mary Margaret would do anything to protect her daughter. She was the only thing that stood between them. She insisted it was too early for him to meet Casey, and there was no way to get Casey on his side if he never had any contact with her. Casey could also decide she was not going to share her mother with any man. Since Dan knew he couldn't get close to her, he had to keep her as far away from her mother as possible. He decided he wanted her out of the way.

"Can't that kid go live with her dad full time?"

"What? Absolutely not. Let me get in my car and you can follow me home." She waited for him to pull up behind her and she started driving home. Mary Margaret called Ben. She put the phone on speaker and left it in her lap. She kept looking in her rearview mirror to make sure Dan wasn't watching her, but he was.

"Ben. Thank God you're home. I need your help. Be at my house in twenty minutes and say something about Casey. It's Dan. He's following me home and I'm scared. OK, thanks, bye."

She pulled in her driveway, Dan parked behind her. She took her time getting inside, pretending to look at the mail. She unlocked the door and Dan pushed in behind her. His hands were all over her, settling in her hair. He pulled her up to his face and said, "who were you talking to in the car, Mary Margaret?" His hands tightened in her hair. "I saw you." He pulled her hair tighter.

"I wasn't talking to anyone. They were playing oldies on the radio, and I was singing. Ow, you're hurting me. Stop it," she demanded.

He pulled back and looked at her with the expression she had no right to demand anything. Dan searched her face trying to decide if she was lying. He decided she was telling the truth and started kissing her again. Mary Margaret kissed him back enough to make him think nothing had changed. He took his hands out of her hair and started to touch her everywhere, his hands roamed her body with impunity.

"Let's go upstairs and fuck."

"We can't. I have to pick up Casey." He grabbed her by the upper arms and shoved her up against the wall and held her there.

"Mary Margaret, here's what you're going to do. You'll send her to live with her father. I'll move in and we can live together. I love you so much I want us to be together all the time. Let's do it. Let's live together. You'd like that, wouldn't you?" He said, squeezing her arms. "After all, if you really loved me, you'd want this, too." The longer she took to answer the harder he tightened his grip.

"Uh, yeah. I have to check with Ben first."

"Wrong answer." He squeezed hard enough to leave her bruised. There was a knock at the door. He released her. "Get rid of them." Mary Margaret went to the door and saw Ben. She opened the door. Ben could tell by the look on her face she needed help. Ben pushed through the doorway and looked at Dan. He nodded his head at Dan and spoke.

"Hey, I just want to make sure you know you need to get Casey. I saw your car in the driveway and thought you might have forgotten. I'd do it, but I have to pick up the cake for Hayes's birthday party. You're still coming, right?"

"Of course. I'm sure Casey would have reminded me. Sorry, Dan, I've got to go. I'll call you later." Ben waited and walked out with them. He made sure that Dan had pulled out and drove off in a different direction. Ben even followed Mary Margaret's car to Casey's school to make sure Dan didn't turn back around and follow her. He was still her best friend, divorced or not.

Ben called her after she safely got Casey, told her to come over and not go home. He didn't trust Dan at all.

They met at his house. It was an unplanned pizza party, the kids excited for an extra visit with their sister and pizza. The kids played, jumping all over the furniture; the adults preoccupied at the table. Sheila was very worried about Mary Margaret. She never quite trusted Dan.

Sheila thought he was exploiting a lonely single mom. He glommed on to her like a drowning man, never giving Mary Margaret a second to breathe. Sheila got her brother Billy Flynn, a detective with the local police on the phone and put it on speaker. They needed a plan to help extract Mary Margaret from the domestic powder keg she found herself sitting atop.

The first thing they needed to do was prevent him from accessing the parking lot at work. Mary Margaret had some pictures of Dan. They were going to print out posters of him, and Billy offered to drop by her parking lot and campus security and have his picture plastered on all the booths, the parking lots and guard shacks, the entrances and exits. They took pictures of her bruises to document her fear of him causing her bodily harm. It was decided Ben would take tomorrow off and shadow Mary Margaret.

They went to the courthouse first thing in the morning to figure out how to get a restraining order against Dan and Ben took her back to work. Ben parked in a reserved handicap spot and walked Mary Margaret to the door, making sure she was safe in case Dan was waiting for her.

At lunch she would meet up again with Ben. Mary Margaret was going to text Dan that it was over and if he contacted her, she was going to get a restraining order. She turned her phone off; Ben took it and got her a new one with a new number. Mary Margaret was on edge all day, fearful of Dan's reaction. He wanted to move in and live together, and she never wanted to see him again.

She thought back over the last few months. Initially, he came on strong, treating Mary Margaret like a prize he couldn't believe he won. Bit by bit he took over her life, not leaving any room for her to think. She found herself giving in rather than expressing her opinion. Her cell phone, he insisted on getting her password and checking it whenever he could. Mary Margaret didn't want to, but he pressured her into telling him.

After all, she had nothing to hide. If she really loved him, she'd do what he wanted. Mary Margaret thought his behavior crossed some line, but he so dominated her thoughts and mind she couldn't think straight and figure out exactly what line. Every time her phone rang, she looked at it like there were two in the chamber. There was no way to gauge his demeanor on the other end if today was the day he'd lose it.

The phrase 'if you really loved me,' he said to her whenever she tried to say no. She gave in under the pressure of his love, if that's what it was. Mary Margaret thought about their sex life. She was never allowed to say no.

In the bedroom her would worship her, telling her all things he knew she wanted to hear. It had been so long since anyone said those things to her; she knew it made her weak and a sucker. He knew that and used it against her. If Casey wasn't home, they had sex. Making love ceased weeks ago. Now, he fucked her.

She recalled how everything was so wonderful in the beginning, how he was with her: totally absorbed. He seduced her using her loneliness and need for affection. He zeroed in on this. It was all so gentle and sweet, she felt cradled in this nest of adoration, only to have him flip the switch.

Dan became forceful and demanding, unwilling to devote the time he used to use to cherish her. He wanted that time spent now on her worshipping him. He became aggressive and unreasonable. Dan took advantage of her desire to please on more than one occasion, leaving her hurt and crying. Her tears meant nothing to him.

Sex used to mean he loved her, and she was special; now he left her feeling used and abused. Mary Margaret couldn't understand how something so beautiful could turn so ugly and violent. What did she do that made him go from kind to cruel? If she said anything, the answer was usually 'it was her own fault.' The harder she tried to make him happy, the more violated she felt.

Mary Margaret was caught in this circle of constantly trying to do better, be better, failing, and being punished for her inability to please him. He was costing her time she wanted to spend with Casey.

He pressured her to do things she didn't want to do, 'if you really loved me, you'd do it,' he said constantly. Mary Margaret wasn't by nature the kind of person who enjoyed conflict, she was laid back and easy going. Dan knew she wouldn't push back on little things; it wasn't worth the fight and drama. Mary Margaret remembered what happened when she stood firm and said no. It was as if he wanted to demonstrate how little control she did have over her own life, over her own body. Mary Margaret laid in bed crying afterward.

"Face it, Mary Margaret," he laughed. "No other man would want you now."

All the little things piled up. Mary Margaret was a prisoner in a cell of her own making. She was so caught up with the little things she lost sight of the big picture. She lost sight of herself, and of Casey, too.

When he wanted her to send Casey to Ben's full-time so he could move in, something in her shifted. The alarm she felt in her head went off in her heart. Mary Margaret had a vision, a moment of clarity of the jam she was in, and she needed to get out of it as soon as possible. She didn't need to break up with him, she needed to escape. Mary Margaret was scared. His reaction would be unpredictable.

Dan was furious she was unreachable by phone. Who was she to tell him it was over and cut off all contact? He would decide if they were finished, not her. Dan wasn't going to wait for her in the parking lot, he would wait outside the building and catch Mary Margaret the minute she left work.

Dan parked in front of her building. Campus Security being what it is was, ineffective at best, didn't stop him. He walked to the door and waited for her, so he could grab her right as she exited the building. She wouldn't be more than two steps away. Dan had it all planned out. He leaned against the wall and waited. Soon he heard the noise of the staff exciting the building. Dan stood up straight, waiting for Mary Margaret.

Things didn't go as Dan planned. First, a tall guy flashing a badge asked him if he was Daniel Bauer. He said yes and the guy hit him in the chest with a piece of folded-up paper.

"Here you go. Make sure you read the fine print," Billy Flynn said. "Have a nice day." He walked off with a wave.

When he looked down at the paper, he was shocked. She got an Emergency Temporary No Contact Order based on her documented bruises and recorded calls of him harassing her. A court date scheduled ten days from today. As the shock registered across his face, Mary Margaret exited; escorted by Ben. She was a few steps ahead of Dan. He ran to her open side and grabbed her arm, trying to stop her.

"Talk to me, Mary Margaret. Now."

Ben crossed in front of her and said, "Hey, Dude. That paper says you are not allowed near her, so back up. About 100 feet." Ben pushed him off and kept her moving. Dan tried to stop her, but Ben wouldn't allow him to touch her and kept her moving forward. They reached her car. Ben stayed between Dan and Mary Margaret. Only when she was safely inside, the door locked and window up, did Ben get the driver's side.

Dan was screaming and pounding on her window. She looked straight ahead. When they pulled away, he was still screaming threats at her. In a sweet twist of Karma, Dan parked his car illegally on campus to get closer to Mary Margaret's building, and while he was waiting for her the University towed his car. It cost him $150 to get it back. Dan wasn't the only who was going to pay. He would make sure Mary Margaret was going to pay, too.

Casey would be staying with Sheila, Ben at Mary Margaret's. She would sleep upstairs, he downstairs on the couch in case Dan decided to pay her a visit. Dan knew if he caused a scene Mary Margaret would invite him rather than have the neighbor's turn on their lights and witness her drama.

Dan came over around 10:30. He had the nerve to park in her driveway. He pounded on her front door yelling for Mary Margaret to let him in, she better let him in, or she'd be sorry. The door opened and Dan tried to push his way in but was met by Ben.

"Dude. Leave. It's over. She's done with you. Do not come back or approach Mary Margaret, or else. The cops are onto you, and if you get near her, she has a direct number to call, and the cops will be on you like white on rice. Take a hint. Beat it if you know what's good for you. It's over," Ben told him and shut the door. Dan left, trying to figure out his next move.

Ben spent the next night over at Mary Margaret's. Dan did not approach her house, and all was silent. Casey was still staying at her dad's; Mary Margaret spent the next night alone with no trouble. She thought Dan took the No Contact Order seriously, there was no reason for Ben to stay. During the day someone from Campus Security met her at the shuttle, escorting her to and from her building.

***

Chapter Four

Mary Margaret saw no sign of Dan despite constantly looking over her shoulder. She parked her car in the garage, put the door down, and entered her house through the kitchen. Once she locked the door, she was able to exhale and finally relax. Mary Margaret felt stressed and worried if she was someplace other than secure in her home. She was on edge and jittery, any loud noise caused her to jump.

On Saturday, Mary Margaret stayed home and did some chores and cooked Casey's favorite dinner, Mustard Chicken. It was in the cookbook under Chicken D'jion, but Casey changed the name when she was younger. Ben was bringing her home later. Mary Margaret sat on the couch and folded clothes when she glanced out the window. Her heart started to race; Dan was sitting in his blue Chevy SUV in front of her house. He sat there all day. Dan left before Ben planned on dropping Casey off. A panicked Mary Margaret called Ben.

"Don't bring her back. He was sitting out front of my house, Ben. In his car. Watching the house."

"Marym, she wants to go back. I'll bring her over and stay for a couple of hours. Let her go to her room, play with her things, get new clothes. I think we should talk to her. She's old enough to know something's going on. Explain why she's staying with us. If Dan continues parking out front, I can talk to Billy and see if there's anything he can do. Make sure you take a picture every time he's out there, so we have proof he's still harassing you."

"Good idea. Stay for dinner. I made her favorite to celebrate her return. How long will this go on, Ben? I'm scared. That court order expires next week. What if he hurts Casey to punish me?"

"He won't. He's a bully, Marym. Any guy that hurts a woman is a coward. I have a feeling he'll leave you alone and find some other girl to harass. We'll go to court and have the order extended. He's supposed show up at court. I bet he doesn't." Big, burly Ben. Steady as a rock. *I guess that's why I married him,* she thought.

Casey came racing in the house and grabbed her mother in a bear hug. "Hi Mom! I miss you."

"I missed you more!" Mary Margaret said, returning the hug. "I made your favorite for dinner. Why don't you go get your things together? You're staying at Daddy's a little bit more."

"I don't want to! I want to stay here! I'm sick of staying at Daddy's. What's going on?"

"We can talk all about it at dinner. You've got fifteen minutes to get your things together before we eat. Hurry upstairs or I'll make you set the table." Casey bolted from the room before her mother finished the sentence. Ben came over and grabbed some plates while Mary Margaret opened the oven door. "Five more minutes. I'll get some glasses," she said and opened a cupboard door. "Ben, how's Sheila doing with this? I'm asking a lot from you guys for an ex-wife."

"She's worried sick about you. Other people may not understand our family, but it works for us. In the age of dysfunctional families, I think ours is one of the most well-adjusted I know." He grabbed the silverware. "That's why we should fill Casey in."

"Ben. It might be too much for her to process. She's in middle school. I don't want her to think the world is an awful place filled with bad people." Mary Margaret wrapped her arms around herself and shivered.

"Too late. It's not all stardust and unicorns. We'll paint her a picture with broad strokes. She's getting older, and she's very bright. We won't get into details unless she asks, and we'll tell her what she wants to know. We just have to stress you're safe. The grown-ups are handling it. It will be fine."

"What will be fine?" Casey asked as she came in and slid into her seat at the table.

"Perfect timing." Mary Margaret said as she put the casserole on the table. Ben sat down, and Mary Margaret took a serving spoon and served everybody.

"Oh, yum. My favorite, Mom. Rice, too." She said, spooning a forkful into her mouth.

"I know."

They ate a few bites and made sounds of pleasure. "Marym, this is your signature dish." Ben told her. "Feel free to bring it by anytime."

"Yeah, Mom. I'm going back to Dad's again. Anybody care to tell me what's going on?"

"Well, honey, it's a grown-up problem, and the grown-ups are handling it, but you're growing up too, so it's only fair you know what's going on. I haven't said anything; I'm afraid I'll scare you and you don't need to worry."

"Scare me? About what?"

Mary Margaret looked at Ben and he nodded, so she continued. "Do you know who Dan is?"

"Yeah. He's that guy that calls you all night when we're trying to hang out. He's so annoying."

"Yes, well, him. I decided I don't want him calling my phone anymore. I don't want to talk to him at all or see him again. Ever. The problem is he doesn't feel the same way and won't stop bothering me. Until he goes away for good, I don't want you here."

"Are you afraid he might hurt me?"

"I'm afraid I don't know what he'll do."

"Are you afraid he'll hurt you?" Casey started to sound nervous, her voice thin and reedy.

"I don't think so. You know how when you're watching a show on TV and its bedtime? And you ask me if you can stay up and watch it until it's over, and I usually say, OK? Or you want to eat ice cream, but it's almost dinner time, and instead of saying 'no you'll ruin your dinner,' I say, OK? I'm kind of push over."

41

"Yeah. You are a push over." Casey said with bit of a smile.

"I don't want to talk to him because I don't want him to try to talk me into changing my mind. I'm done with him. He showed up at my work. Your Dad stayed over a few nights just in case he came over and made noise. Today he parked out front and stayed there all afternoon. He's unpredictable and don't want you around until he's gone for good."

"Maybe you shouldn't be here either." Casey said, sounding uneasy.

"You are growing up. That's a good point." Mary Margaret said. "Unfortunately, I have deal with him. I don't want to be looking over my shoulder the rest of my life. I think he might need more than 'thanks, it's been real. Bye.' That's why your dad is involved. He told him to get lost. We went to court and got a no contact order. If he doesn't respect that, your Uncle Billy will get involved. He'll pay him a visit and tell him if he doesn't stop, the entire police force is going to get involved. Personally, I think he thinks he knows me, and if he gets close enough to talk to me, I'll cave. He took advantage of me when I was feeling lonely. I look at your dad and Sheila and how happy they are; I wanted that for myself. But not with him. He's the wrong guy. He's gotta go. He'll get the message." Mary Margaret tried to sound firm and confident.

"You really think so?" Casey asked, wanting to believe her mother.

"Yes, I do. He's a bully, and bullies are usually cowards. Once he gets the message, he'll find some other girl to take advantage of."

"That's not fair to her."

"No, it's not, but I can't worry about her. I've got to handle my own shit."

Casey looked at her mother, surprised she swore. Mary Margaret tried to never swear in front of her daughter. Maybe they did recognize she was growing up.

"Believe it or not there are girls who would be into a guy who became obsessed with them. That's not me. I have other things in my life I'd rather pay attention to, like you. Nobody comes ahead you, and he wanted to be the center of my world. Well, even if you weren't here, I wouldn't want some guy to totally dominate me. I think I got carried away with all the attention. It was very flattering, but I realized it wasn't at all what I wanted. Now I'm in over my head and need help getting away from him. I'm doing it with the help of your dad and Uncle Billy. So don't worry about it. He'll get the message."

"You sound like you have it all planned out. What if he doesn't stop?

"I've thought about that too. If worse comes to worse, I'll ask Uncle Billy for the name of someone who isn't necessarily a good guy, and hire him to beat the shit out of Dan. I'll hire him to be my bodyguard. Dan will get the message one way or the other, so don't worry. Your dad is helping me."

"OK, I'll trust you guys to handle it. Thanks for telling me. I knew something was going on. I'm not stupid." Casey told her parents.

"We know that but didn't want to worry you. I didn't want you looking over your shoulder, too. It isn't about you."

"Yeah, it is. You're my mother. So now I know. Think of it this way: you have another pair of eyes looking out for you." Casey said with a nod, satisfied she knew the score. She grabbed the spoon and piled more on her plate. "This is so good, Mom. Did I tell you Courtney got grounded because she lied about failing a math test? The teacher called before Courtney got home."

It took the three of them no time at all to clean up after dinner. Casey got her things together as they prepared to leave. She kissed her mom on the cheek. "Goodbye, Mother. Don't forget to set the alarm after we leave. Keep me posted and be safe."

"I will, sweetie. Don't worry, your Dad and I are taking care of things. Bye, Ben. I'll see you Wednesday."

"What's Wednesday?"

"We go back to court." Ben said, now that Casey was in the loop she deserved to know.

Casey looked at her parents, glad they were honest with her. Maybe her family wasn't like others, but it worked for them. "Don't forget to set the alarm." She told her mother again.

"Will do," Mary Margaret said as they left. She set the alarm and went upstairs. Mary Margaret read in bed for a while and turned off the light. Before she turned in for the night, she looked out the window. The street was quiet and vacant of parked cars. She got in bed and went to sleep, her mind at peace.

***

She awoke the next morning, the first thing she did was check out front and look for Dan, but the street was the same as the night before. Mary Margaret made a cup of coffee and turned on her computer. She looked at the day's news and checked her email. When Dan was around, she hid her laptop. She didn't want him to know she had one, and check it liked he did her phone. Dan was more interested in her contacts and texts. When he asked about her email, she said she used the one at work. He never asked about it again and she never told him her address. Mary Margaret had created a dummy account years ago, mostly for places that asked for an address, and she knew it'd be a likely source of spam. If he insisted on one, that would be the one she would have given him.

She spent the rest of the morning cleaning out closets. Mary Margaret was surprised by the amount of stuff she had. She didn't realize the closets were so deep. A lot of things were coats and shoes of Casey's she outgrew before they had a chance to wear out. She packed it all in garbage bags to donate to Goodwill. *There's going to be one well-dressed little girl out there.* Mary Margaret thought. She was so conscientious she felt obligated to match each pair of footwear and rubber band them together before donating them. She dragged the bags into the garage, opened her trunk, and loaded them in her car.

"There." She said to herself. "Now I can watch TV for the rest of the day and not feel guilty."

Mary Margaret made a sandwich, grabbed a soda and sat on the couch. All that cleaning put her in the mood to watch Hoarders. She took the remote and bounced around the channels until she found one running a Hoarders marathon. A shadow passed by the front window so quickly she wasn't sure she actually saw something. The hair on the back of her neck stood up and she got a queasy feeling deep in the pit of her stomach. She crept over to look out the window without being seen, and she saw Dan sitting in his car in front of her

44

house. *Fuck. Was he walking around her house?* She thought. Mary Margaret got her phone and took a picture.

A switched flipped inside her. She was done being afraid of feeling like a victim. She called Ben but wanted to speak with Sheila and get Billy Flynn's number. She was taking matters into her own hands.

"Billy Flynn," he answered.

"Hi, Billy, it's me, Ben's ex-wife, Mary Margaret. You were helping me with that guy who won't take no for an answer."

"Yes. He still bothering you?"

"Yeah. He's been parked in front of my house for hours, and I think he was walking around my yard. Do you have anybody out on patrol? If they aren't busy, could they drive by my house every once in a while? I live on Greenleaf Terrace. He has a blue Chevy SUV parked in front of my house and he's sitting in it."

"I'll do you one better. I'm nearby. I'll pay him a visit."

"I don't want to inconvenience you. It doesn't have to be now, but I want to let him know the police are aware of him."

"I'll swing by now. It'll be fun."

"Thanks, Billy. I owe you big."

"It's my job, 'To Protect and Serve,' so you're keeping me in business."

Mary Margaret laughed. "Thanks, Billy."

Five minutes later, Billy turned down her street, the blue Chevy the only car parked on the side of the road. He pulled up alongside it, put his car in park and got out. He tapped on the window, and Dan lowered it. "Yes?" He said rudely, looking at Billy. *What a dick,* Billy thought and flashed his badge.

"Hey, Buddy. What are you doing? A few of the neighbors called in a complaint of a strange car being parked on the street. A lady walking her dog said she knows everybody who lives on this block, and you don't. So, I ask again, what are you doing parked here, and if I have to ask a third time, you won't be happy."

"Nothing. My girlfriend lives in that house." Dan gave Billy a look and dismissed him, like he was a door-to-door salesman selling encyclopedias. Billy's badge meant nothing. He was in the right he could sit there all day if he wanted. This was a public road, and that cowboy cop couldn't do anything about it.

"Wrong answer. See, that's the thing about a small town, everybody knows everybody else's business. Your girlfriend there? I think you mean your ex-girlfriend. I think she told you in no uncertain terms it's over."

"We're just having a fight and she overreacted. I'm just waiting for her to calm down."

"Wrong again. I know that because she's family. She's part of a *cop's* family, and you don't fuck around with a member of a *cop's* family. Not if you want to lead a peaceful life."

"Look. I know my rights and I pay my taxes. This is a public street, and I don't see a 'No Parking' sign. I'm not bothering anybody and I'm not breaking any laws. You've got nothing." Dan said.

"Well. I guess you told me," Billy said and gave him his business card. "Take care, now." He walked slowly back, got in his car and drove away. Ten minutes later, a patrol car pulled up. The officer got out and approached him. Dan was ready. He had his window down and watched the cop walk up in his side mirror.

"License and registration, sir."

"Look. Like I told the other cop, I'm not doing anything wrong."

"License and registration." The officer didn't say 'sir' this time.

Dan got out his wallet and handed them over. "Go ahead. You won't find anything."

The officer walked back and sat in his car for a bit and sat there a bit more. He got out and walked back to Dan's car. Dan's patience was almost gone. First, the

46

other guy, and now this one. He stuck his hand out the window to take back his paperwork. "See." He spoke. "Nothing."

"Not exactly. Here's your license and registration. Here's a ticket for loitering."

"But..but..you gotta be kidding me!" Dan got red in the face and louder. "This is harassment!"

"Tell it to the judge. Court date is on the bottom. Have a good day." He got in his cruiser and drove off. Dan sat in his car and fumed. What the fuck is Mary Margaret trying to do? She knows better. He sat in his car and got mad and madder still. Dan got so mad he got out of his car and stormed up the walk and started pounding on Mary Margaret's front door.

"Open this door immediately! Who the fuck do you think you are? You let me in, you bitch, if you know what's good for you! You'll be sorry! Open this door now! You'll pay for this, Mary Margaret, I swear to God you'll pay!" He screamed and continued to rage outside her door. Soon the cop car returned. The officer got out with a grim look on his face and walked up to Dan.

"OK, buddy. That's enough of that. You're going to have to come with me." He grabbed Dan's arm to turn him away from the door. Dan wrenched his arm out of the policeman's grasp.

"Get your hands off of me! Don't touch me again! This is harassment!"

"No, it's resisting arrest and violation of a no contact order. It might even be considered trespassing and causing a public nuisance." The officer said calmly, with an undercurrent of you don't want to take this further in his voice.

"There's no fucking way I'm going with you. You can't do this!"

"Watch me," the officer said, and in one swift move he turned Dan face first towards the door, shoved him; and pinned him against the door with his shoulder. Maybe he didn't need to, but the officer made sure Dan's face was smushed up tight against Mary Margaret's front door. He already had one of Dan's arms bent painfully behind him, he cuffed him in one smooth motion. The policeman turned Dan around and escorted him into the back seat of his patrol car, all the while Dan cursed and spewed obscenities at the cop. Before placing him in the backseat, he asked, "Mr. Bauer, have you been drinking?" Dan responded with more curses and four-letter words, this time including threats against Mary Margaret.

"I guess I can add drunk and disorderly, and I'll be writing in my report you made multiple threats against the resident of this house who has an a No Contact Order on file against you. So, if I were you, I'd shut my mouth. Watch your head there, sir." The officer said as he none too gently placed Dan into his car and took him downtown.

Mary Margaret watched them drive off and finally took a deep breath. She didn't realize the tension she was holding within her until she saw Dan really was gone. She took pictures of the whole incident to take to court with her on Wednesday. Mary Margaret wondered if she should have a lawyer present so Dan would feel the full weight of what would happen to him if he didn't leave her alone. Now that he was gone, she felt comfortable enough to leave her house. She felt an overwhelming desire to see Casey, to make sure she was OK. She drove over to Ben's, stopping first at a liquor store to buy a bottle of wine.

"I come bearing good news. Dan got carted off my front steps in handcuffs. He went to the police station in the back of a cop car. Billy Flynn helped so much. After I talked to you, we spoke. He dropped by, talked to him and left. Then a police car pulls up, hassles him for a bit and leaves. Dan came up to my door pounding, screaming, yelling threats at me.

"The cop comes back, they have words, and he gets taken away in handcuffs. They even towed away his car! I don't need you to come with me on Wednesday, Ben; I'm taking my lawyer. He needs to get involved and make sure all things legal-like get taken care of legally."

"If you say so, Marym, if you say so," Ben said.

"I do, Ben, I do."

On Wednesday, she went with her lawyer to court. To her surprise Dan appeared as well as Billy Flynn and the arresting officer. When it was her turn, they went before the judge. Her lawyer laid out what had happened.

When it was Dan's turn the judge asked him for his version of the events; he didn't deny being at her house. He didn't deny threatening her. Dan was there because the cops were harassing him. He wanted them to reimburse the cost of getting his car out of the impound lot. Dan said the officer wrenched his arm back so hard he had to go to the doctor for his injured shoulder. He submitted his bills.

"Anything else either side would like to submit before I make my ruling?"

Mary Margaret spoke up. "Yes. I have a young daughter who can't live with me because I'm afraid to bring her home. It's not safe. She can't be exposed to Dan Bauer and his threats. I fear he might retaliate by harming her. Here are pictures of some of the bruises from when he assaulted me."

The judge signaled the bailiff to bring them up. He took a quick glance at them. The judge thought Dan Bauer was the worse type of guy: someone who preyed on the weakness of others. A man who thought he had the right to exploit those unlucky enough to cross his path. *Not in my courtroom,* he thought.

"God damn it, Mary Margaret! I don't know what you're trying to pull but you won't get away with it!" Dan exploded.

"Mr. Bauer, that outburst did you no favor. You threatened her in front of a judge. I have no other option but to extend the No Contact Order for an additional thirty days. If I see you here again, I'll issue a restraining order against you. I recommend some anger management classes. You seem to have a problem with your temper. Maybe even counseling. Ms. Welch doesn't love you anymore and you can't seem to accept it."

"Counseling? Anger Management? You're crazy." Dan said to the judge.

"Well, Mr. Bauer, again that outburst did you no good. I have no other recourse but to find you in contempt. Bailiff, escort Mr. Bauer to the holding cell. He needs some time to think before he speaks. Mr. Bauer, I suggest you use the time to reflect on your behavior. You need to think about how to act in a court of law, and how to treat women."

Mary Margaret left the courtroom and waited outside for her lawyer. Dan was further down the hall, the deputy who was escorting him stopped to talk to someone. He saw Mary Margaret, broke away from the officer and ran towards her screaming. He made it about three feet when one of the officers rammed his elbow into Dan's chest, pinning him against the wall. Two others escorted him down the hall as he raged and screamed threats against Mary Margaret.

"I'll get you, you bitch!" Dan screamed.

"You're being charged with assault, resisting arrest, and any other charge I can think of." The deputy whose job was originally to transport Dan was pissed. The other officers took him away, still hissing and cursing.

"I'm sorry, ma'am. There was a hold-up in processing, and I didn't realize you were still in the building."

"Maybe what happened was a good thing."

"Excuse me, ma'am. I'm not following."

"I'm pressing charges. Assault, domestic violence, jaywalking, I don't fucking care. Oh, excuse me," she said. "I shouldn't use foul language. If he gets charged he'll have to get a lawyer. I'm holding all the cards. If he wants to get his ass out of hot water he'll have to behave himself. I never want to see or speak to him again. He won't listen to me. Maybe he'll listen to you."

"If he doesn't, I can assure you he won't be able to go ten feet without being stopped for some infraction, real or alleged. I understand you're related to Detective Billy Flynn."

"Yes," Mary Margaret said. "By marriage." *Kinda. Sorta.*

"Good guy to have in your corner."

Her lawyer came out and they left. Mary Margaret felt a weight lift off her chest. She had no idea how the stress of it all affected her until it was gone.

***

Tall, long-boned, his rust-colored hair neat and cut close to his head, Billy Flynn stopped by to see Mary Margaret after Dan's brother had to pick up Dan from jail. "'You got caught stalking some girl again, didn't you,' his brother was overheard saying." Billy Flynn laughed at that. "If you see him anywhere, call me. Please."

"You know, the name Billy Flynn conjures up the stereotypical Irish cop, years of hard living and harder drinking, belly protruding over his belt, a polyester suit coat wearing, barstool sitting cop. Facial features lumpy like a baked potato." Mary Margaret said.

"All that?"

"Don't interrupt me." She censured him. "Now what was I talking about? Oh, you. You're the antithesis of the stereotype. What do you do, run marathons? Hike the Five Peaks?"

He was married, had two kids, and ran for an hour each day as an excuse to get out of his house and get some peace.

"Your poor wife."

"When I get home, I take care of everything, and she gets an hour to do whatever she's into."

"Sounds reasonable," Mary Margaret said.

"The only thing that bothers me is my face might look like a lumpy potato. No amount of running can fix that."

"It doesn't. Maybe you didn't slather yourself in baby oil and lay in the sun for hours when you were a teenager."

"No, I did not. I played a lot of baseball, but wore a cap."

"That explains it, then."

Billy Flynn unfolded his limbs and stood up. "I'm glad Dan Bauer didn't get enough time to fuck up your head. That's what happens in a lot of these cases, the guy's a jerk, the girl thinks she can 'fix' him with enough love. But he's not a jerk, he's a horrible, awful, man that destroys a woman one chunk at a time.

"By the time she realizes she's in a bad place, she's compromised so much of herself she doesn't know how to fight back. Somewhere along the way she has a baby. Maybe because she thought it would 'help' things, or maybe he pressured her into it, but now she's chained to him. But I'm glad you realized what a bad guy he really is before he caused too much damage."

"I don't think I can close the book on this and walk away, so no harm, no foul. He did fuck up my head." Mary Margaret admitted. "I don't know if I'll ever stop looking over my shoulder. I don't know if I'll ever not worry about my daughter when she's not with me or wonder if I can trust my own judgment again. Or trust other people and not question their motives. I can't imagine going through life now not being scared of something bad and not recognizing it until it's too late."

"I can see that. Talk to a professional to help you process it all. I highly recommend it. If you don't, he'll win. Don't give him that. Please. Call the station and get the name of someone who works with women who survive domestic violence. You may not have had a black eye or broken arm but abuse always starts with head games." He said as he stood up. "Anyway, I will see you at the next family function, cousin. Goodbye, Mary Margaret. I'll see you around, but never again in this capacity."

"Thank you, Billy. Huh. Thank you, Billy Flynn. There. That sounds better. I don't know what I would have done without your help. It scares me to think about all the other women without the access to the resources I had. If my husband fell in love with somebody other than Sheila, I'd be just like them."

"No you wouldn't. You'd find a way to get out, even if you had to kill him in his sleep if it meant saving yourself and your kids."

"I could never do that. I'm not that kind of person."

"You never know what you're capable of until you feel trapped with no escape. File this under 'lesson learned the hard way,' and move on. Goodbye, Mary Margaret. I have to go now. I can show myself out."

52

Mary Margaret did see a therapist for a while and work through her emotions; it took time to decompress from the situation. No matter how much she tried to forgive herself for being so weak and needy, there was something down deep that she couldn't let go of that made her feel it was a mess of her own making. She should have trusted her gut and got the hell out of there.

Chapter Five

It took Mary Margaret a long time to stop being scared. Scared wasn't the word. Spooked was the word. The therapist told her it was a form of PTSD, her nervous system conditioned to be on high alert. It didn't take much for the fight or flight hormones to kick in. She couldn't believe only a few short months in a situation like that could wreak such havoc. Mary Margaret wondered about women exposed to such stress on a daily basis; how they managed to survive.

One day she realized she had stopped looking under every rock and around every corner for danger. She relaxed and fell into a smooth groove of motherhood and family. Casey grew into a sharp, smart, intelligent young woman with a quick wit.

Marym closely watched Casey grow up but tried to do it from a distance. She kept involved, like working the Snack Shack at games that had nothing to with daughter, so when she happened to be there at one of boy's soccer games and Casey showed up, it was purely in the role of a Booster Club Mom.

Marym saw Dan once from her car, in the parking lot of the grocery store. She drove right by him and he didn't notice her. He had his arm around the shoulder of a young, doe eyed girl who gazed up at him in adoration. She didn't seem to mind the possessive nature of his embrace. Marym felt bad about the young girl, she wanted to warn her. She hoped the girl had a couple of older brothers who would pound the crap out of Dan if he stepped out of line, but the girl looked like she liked belonging to someone. Marym drove out of the parking lot and headed for home. She finally felt free.

***

Mary Margaret hadn't seen John since he left after they had coffee and donuts. She thought about him a bit more than she wanted to, and decided any guy that walked away that easily was a wimp and not worth her time. John didn't strike her as a wimp. He was probably a mature, well-adjusted man who didn't chase women who told him they weren't interested.

It wasn't a matter of being interested and playing hard-to-get; she never played those games because she never understood the rules. Mary Margaret figured any average, healthy guy wouldn't be attracted to her; she emitted some signal that was a beacon for nut jobs and wackos.

John left Marym alone, not because he wasn't interested, but because he was. Mary Margaret shut him down before he even said anything. If that's the way she felt, he had to respect it. He wondered, though, if it was really the way she felt or just a reflex she developed to keep the world at bay.

For some reason he didn't understand she presented with such a tough exterior. John was curious how deep that ran. Was it because she really was a tough old bird, or was it merely a shell she developed for protection? John didn't like the way his preoccupation with Mary Margaret ran below the surface like a news crawl did across the bottom of a TV screen.

John saw her once at the park, he was running, and she was walking Stella. John thought about changing his route to 'accidentally' cross her path, but Mary Margaret hurt his feelings the last time he saw her. He made sure he went in the opposite direction.

John ran into Casey one day at the coffee shop. He was ordering when he saw her sitting at a table alone, a pile of books in front of her. He asked the server if he knew what she ordered, he did so John ordered one for her as an excuse to talk to her.

"Hello, Casey. I've brought you another coffee. Judging from the number of books in front of you, I thought you might be ready for a break, or more fuel." He extended the cup to her when she looked up, a blank look on her face. "It's John. I met you at the hospital when your mother came in for stitches." She smiled and reached for the coffee.

"Oh, right, right. John. A break, definitely. Have a seat."

"How are you? You look knee deep in textbooks. Are you back in school?"

"Yeah. I'm studying to be Nurse Practitioner. Being an R.N. Is great, but I can't see being a grunt the rest of my life. It's a grind on you. Physically, you beat the crap out of your body caring for incapacitated people twice your size, you screw up your body clock with the messed-up hours. Mentally, you get old and bitter because a lot of your patients shouldn't be patients. Lose some weight, take a walk, check your blood pressure. It doesn't take much, but people don't seem to get it. How are you doing, John?"

"Good. Work. Golf. A run in the park. A day in the life," John said.

"C'mon. You know you want to," Casey said with a laugh.

"Want to what?"

"Ask about my mother."

"Busted. Am I that transparent?"

"It was either her or Stella. My mother's better looking." Casey teased.

"Yeah, but Stella's nicer. How's your mom's eye?"

"Why don't you ask her yourself?"

"She told me to go away. So, I'm away." He said with a shrug of his shoulders.

"So go visit Stella. Bring her a bone."

"I'm afraid your mom will give her one of mine, and I still need them."

Casey laughed again. "Yeah, that sounds like her, but I'll let you in on a little secret. She's a marshmallow. A creampuff. Stella's more likely to bite you than she is."

"I don't believe we're talking about the same person. Your mother has some sharp edges. Why?"

She sat back and looked at John, trying to assess how much information about her mother she wanted to disclose. "I'm not sure I'm comfortable talking about my mom. She's a very private person, but it bothers me she puts this face out there that she's somebody she's not."

56

"Casey. I mean your mom no harm. In fact, quite the opposite. I kinda like her. I just don't understand her. If you don't want to share details about her, that's fine. I can respect that."

"I normally wouldn't. I'd say go ask her yourself, but for some reason I'd like to help you. Maybe because you helped her. I can tell you what I think, if it'll help. I don't think my mom has had a very successful track record as far as relationships go. I mean look at her and my Dad. She loved him, he loved her. They still love each other, for Christ's sake. But as friends. Best friends. She explains it as she didn't have a lot of experience with love, and she thought being in love meant marrying your best friend. So did my dad.

"When he met Sheila, a light bulb went off as to what romantic love was all about, and he still loved my mom, but not that way, not the way you're supposed to if you're married. So, I think it kind of rocked her that everything she thought was right was wrong. I remember when I was in elementary school, she saw someone for a while, I think she liked him too. I guess one night he told her he was going back to his wife, so she thought she called that one wrong, too.

"I think the final straw came when she got involved with some guy when I was in middle school. I remember this because I hated him. I never met him, my mom was good about keeping me separate, but from what I recall, he sucked her in so quick and deep she mistook it as that grand passion that caused my dad to leave her.

"It wasn't passion; it was an obsession. Domination. He was a master manipulator, my stepmother said, and thinks he found her weaknesses and exploited the shit out of her. Personally, I think he was abusive. If it wasn't physical, it sounded like it was headed that way.

"I had to stay at my dad's because she wanted to keep me away from him; he kept showing up and harassing her. He even showed up at her work. In order to get him to leave her alone the cops got involved and she had to go to court and everything. It took her a long time to accept he was really gone. For a while it was like he was going to show up at any moment; she was so tense all the time, but eventually she relaxed. But here again, she thought it was her fault, that she misread the situation.

"As far as I know, that's been her love life. She once said to me 'three strikes and I'm out.' I took that to mean she was done with men, I guess. She stopped trying, or maybe she stopped looking. I kind of feel like a traitor, talking behind my mom's back like this. She might have a different version of events.

"I was a little kid so I'm not sure how accurate my impressions are. I do know that last guy, she and my dad told me what was going on and how they were handling the situation because I was asking questions. But, yeah, that's her story. Or how I see it, but again, I could be totally wrong."

John sat back and digested what Casey told him. He wasn't sure what to think. It did sound like love had certainly put Mary Margaret through the wringer. He could feel the anger rise the more he thought about it. From his point of view, she deserved none of it. "Thank you, Casey. I think you've helped me understand why she's so prickly."

"Prickly? That's a good word for it. My mom has done a great job preserving the mother/child dynamic. She's never leaned on me or involved me in any of her drama. She's never expected me to be a substitute spouse, a little adult or confidant. I hope she isn't mad."

She stopped talking and looked at John. He could sense there was more, but wasn't sure Casey was comfortable with sharing it. *I don't know why I suddenly shared all that; it's my mom's story to tell, not mine. I guess you caught me at an opportune moment, sitting here working on my future.*

"To be honest, I'm being selfish. I went through the University's nursing school. I work at University Hospital. I don't live with my parents I live with two other nurses. We have a flat near the hospital. Here is the only place I've ever lived. I think when I finish up my degree, I might want to leave and see what else the world has to offer."

"If my mom knew I stayed here because I was concerned about her, she'd be seriously pissed. She's made it clear she is not my responsibility, and I know that. I can't help that I worry about her. Maybe if she had more friends, I wouldn't feel so bad about wanting to leave here."

"You're supposed to want to leave," John said after he sipped his coffee. "You're young; it's your job to leave and strike out on your own. It must be different with girls; I have two boys and never expected them to come back after college and put down roots. They grew up outside of Philadelphia, but if they settled there because of their parents, they'd be alone.

"After my wife and I split up, there was no home to go back to. I travel for work, so wherever my contract is, that's my home until the next assignment. My one son is in Dallas, that's where my ex ended up. She followed him. My other son is outside of D.C. I'd be happy to be friends with your mom, but I'm not sure she wants to be friends with me. By the way, how is her eye?"

"Sorry, John, but you'll have to ask her yourself. My lips are sealed."

"Oh, so now you're not talking."

"Nope. You're on your own. I must insist you go. I have to work tonight and need to get my paper written. Run along," she dismissed him. He stood up.

"I'll go, but before I do can I get you anything else?"

"Nope. I'm good, but I really have to finish this before my shift starts."

"Casey, you work too hard. Leave yourself some time for fun."

"Fun? I'd be happy with a good night's sleep. Bye, John." She put her head down and went back to her books.

John went outside and sat in his car but didn't start it. He turned over in his mind what Casey shared with him. By this point in their lives, most adults have been casualties of love gone bad with the scars to prove it; but it seemed to him every time Mary Margaret thought she was happy love bit her in the right in the ass. No wonder she was so guarded.

He decided he would stop by and check out her eye, but he needed to stop by the grocery store. John wanted to get Stella a ham bone. The butcher didn't have one, and the only way to get one was to buy a ham and have the butcher trim the meat off. It cost him fifty bucks, but he walked out of there with a ham bone.

He pulled into Mary Margaret's driveway and parked next to this big, black late model truck. John didn't consider it a monster truck, but it was close. He wasn't sure who she had for company, but he was sure he didn't want to meet the guy who drove it. Either it was a lumberjack who couldn't fit into anything else, or a regular guy with a little dick and a big chip on his shoulder.

Neither option looked good, but he went through all this to get Stella a bone, so he'd drop it off and run. The garage door was up, but he wasn't sure if he should knock at the inside door or be formal and go up to the front door. He decided any woman who made him think this much might be too much for him.

Once again, she made the decision for him. Mary Margaret came out the door that exited from the kitchen into the garage.

"Jason. It's about time. I've been waiting almost an hour for you." She looked up John and said "Oh. It's you." She blinked her eyes a few times like he might be a mirage.

John was sure if she was happy to see him, she'd smile at him or some other positive expression. Instead, she looked at him warily. She looked at him like she'd look if she found a python curled up on the floor of her garage. No immediate threat, but unsure of how to proceed. He took the lead, remembering what Casey said.

"Hi. Yes, it is me. I won't stay; I just wanted to see how your eye healed." He looked at her eye. She was even prettier than he thought, maybe it was the absence of a black eye, but she healed nicely. Stella barked, and barked some more. Mary Margaret opened the door up; the little dog went over to John and sat. She whined a bit and thumped her tail expectantly. John looked down at the little dog and smiled. At least the dog was happy to see him. "Why, hello, Stella. How are you girl?" The dog looked excitedly at him.

"That's odd. She seems extremely glad to see you. Usually, she's a little bit more reserved around strangers."

"I've walked her a few times. I'm not a stranger to her." John said. "She knows I have a present for her, don't you, Stella? I brought her a bone. Is it ok if I give it to her? It's a ham bone, so I don't think it will splinter; but she's your dog so it's your call."

"I think if I don't give it to her, she'll never forgive me," Mary Margaret said. "Let's see it."

John took the bone out of the bag and unwrapped the butcher's paper. It was pretty big, about as long as Stella.

"Is it OK if I give it to her?" She laughed at the size of the bone and the excitement of Stella.

"Sure. It's almost as big as she is, but I'm sure she'll find a way to manage." Her phone rang, and she took her attention away from John giving the bone to Stella. *I went through all this trouble to make a positive impression, and she's not even looking this way,* he thought and gave the bone to the dog. She gnawed at it a few times trying to find a way to fit it in her mouth. She was finally able to grab hold of the fascia that connected the meat to the bone and proceeded to drag it out onto the lawn. She got comfortable in the grass and settled in for the kind of bliss only a bone could give a dog. John turned back to Mary Margaret, ready to say goodbye, but she was still on the phone. He listened to her half of the conversation. He gathered this must be Jason's truck.

"Jesus, Jason. Tell her to stop crying and get over here. I need your help." She paused while Jason talked. "Why the hell did you do that? How could you be so stupid?" Another pause. "I guess. I can try Casey, but I think she's busy. Let me see what I can do. If I can't get anyone you'll have to just bring her and she can cry in your car. OK. Bye." She hung up and looked at John. "Are you busy for the next couple hours? My helper has girl trouble. Apparently he called his new girlfriend his old girlfriend's name and she's have's having a meltdown."

"That's not good. I'm free if you need someone to help. What's going on?" John said.

"I have to go to The Warehouse and pick up a few things. It's a couple of canvases; they're not heavy, but large."

"I can do that."

She walked over to the truck and opened the driver's side door. "Hop in."

John opened the passenger door and climbed in. He looked admiringly at the inside of the truck. It had every feature ever offered in a car, or a truck. "Wow. This is quite a truck. I'm surprised Jason lets you drive it."

She started the truck and pulled out of her driveway. "Why do you think it's Jason's?"

"I thought you had company. A lumberjack or the Incredible Hulk. It's a dude's dream truck. It's yours?"

She nodded yes.

"Why you bad ass motherfucker." John said, figuring she'd enjoy the compliment.

She laughed at that. "That's me."

John felt inordinately pleased he made her laugh. He needed to keep her good mood from evaporating. He figured the truck and their errand were safe subjects. "How'd you end up with a truck like this?"

"I bought it off of a friend of Jason's. He bought it, had it for a while, and realized he wanted to move to Colorado. He needed to sell it in order to leave; he couldn't afford the payments. I needed a truck, so I helped him out and paid off his note, and I got a truck. I was going to sell it, it's way more truck than I need, but I kind of like driving it. I'm up high and people get out of my way."

"Why do you need a truck?"

"I have a studio down at the Warehouse, and sometimes have oversized canvases I need moved. That's why I wanted a truck."

"Where's the Warehouse?"

"The Warehouse?" She looked at him. "Oh, that's right, you're not from around here. The Warehouse used to be a warehouse for a furniture company. They moved to a new place in the suburbs, and the building was left vacant.

"For a while it was abandoned, and squatters took over, until there was a fire. It was boarded up and fenced in, a real eyesore. The city was going to tear it down, but the Council of the Arts got a grant, and any artist interested in leasing space would get a break on the rent if they helped rehab it.

"The grant covered the structural and plumbing and the big things, the rest of us painted and did all the cosmetic stuff. When the ceiling started leaking on the upper floor, we got a roofer it come in and fix it. He donated the labor we passed the hat around town and got the materials. The roofer had a kid who was in a thrash metal band that used a studio. I think he wanted to keep the band out of his garage, so that's why he got involved.

"Same thing with the freight elevator. Those of us on the upper floors couldn't access our space and carry our materials up the stairs, so somebody knew somebody who knew some guy who worked for an elevator company. Same thing. They donated labor and we scrounged up the money for the rest. It's not in the greatest location, so somebody knew somebody else who installed a security system, outside cameras, and all that, but we had to fence in the parking lots. The city gave us money for that." She paused, distracted by a car that pulled out in front of them. One second later, and that car would have been squished so flat it could be used as a coaster.

"Asshole, " she said of the driver, seconds from death. "Where was I? Oh, yeah. I think the elected officials were pleased that we took that building five minutes from being condemned to a functional place for creative use. A gallery opened on the bottom floor as well as a small theater. In the back there's a spot for live shows. There's even a coffee shop with a stage for poetry slams and all that open on weekends. It's been good. The city got a pat on the back for wise use of public grants. The under forty crowd, many of them creative types, needed studio space stuck around. To their parent's delight or dismay, I'm not sure which. We even welcomed cops.

"There's an effort to humanize the police. They are there with cars and uniforms before scheduled events. Partly to communicate no shit would be tolerated, partially as an act of goodwill. They wished people good luck. Sometimes they could get who was performing out of one of the many groups of kids who passed by to engage, and it's nice. One trooper brought a cadaver dog. Anything to get people to see the popo as regular people.

"Whoever designed the fence made it nine feet tall, so it felt like you were inside an outside space rather than fenced in. And I talked all the way here because here it is."

Mary Margaret pulled up to the fence and got out, walked over and opened the lock. She opened up the gates and pulled her truck in; getting out to lock up behind them. Mary Margaret pulled around the other side. There was a larger door which opened. Because the outer gate was secure, they could prop the door open to load and unload stuff and not worry.

She opened the freight elevator, and they rode up to the third floor. When they exited the elevator John looked around. There were wood floor hallways that went in different directions. Each hallway was lined with doors that opened into the individual studios. The doors were all closed, and it was like they were the only people in the building.

"Wow," John said. "This place is pretty cool. It's so quiet."

"Yeah, until the bands start up. Those studios are on the first floor. They're supposed to be sound proof, but it still can be loud. It's too early for them."

John followed her to one of the closed doors. There was a painting of Godzilla tacked to her door. He looked at the poster.

"Does Godzilla have a special meaning?" John asked.

"That's Jason. He hung that up and calls this 'The Godzilla Col-lab Studio.'"

"Why?"

"I don't know. He said because it's cool. We don't Col-Laborate on anything either."

"Wow. This is cool," he said looking around.

"That's Jason's side. My stuff is over here. She went behind a shower curtain, and around another. It opened up to a large open area with a window that let in the daylight. She had a wide table, made out of plywood and sawhorses in the middle of her space. There was a shallow box made out of plywood, too, the size of the table about six inches deep inverted atop, hiding whatever lay underneath. She uncovered canvases leaning against the walls, categorized in a system that existed only in her head. Mary Margaret pulled four large canvases and a few of the smaller ones. She approached the table and asked him to come over.

"Here. Help me take this top off. On the count of three, lift it straight up about a foot, and hold it." After they did that, she said, "Ok, we're heading over to the right until we clear the table at which point, we tip it vertical and lean it against the wall."

Underneath was a large 2'x4' canvas; it was a large abstract of all colors of deep blue swirled with white and silver poking through the dark with a finish like glass.

"What do you think?"

"It's like looking out of the window of the space shuttle."

"Perfect. I work with a couple of realtors who stage homes. This is drama on a budget. Cheap thrills."

"What do you mean?"

"I can knock a couple of these out a day. The problem is finding space to dry them flat. Same for the finish. That's for a little boy's room, the theme is 'Space.' There's also two smaller ones. One's round, like a window. The other three are just accents. Oh, and one that sits atop a mantle. The key is keeping them from getting damaged in transit, which is why the sheets and pillowcases. It took the three trips to load them satisfactorily.

She said, "Hey, John. You want to drive?" Mary Margaret tossed him the keys without waiting for an answer. He nodded excitedly and got in the driver's side. He luxuriated in the comfort it provided.

"Oh, man." He sighed.

"Drive up to the gate, I'll get out and do the gate, you pull through. I'll lock up." He did as he was told. She climbed back in.

"Where to?"

"On the east side. Near Bridges High school."

"Remember, I'm not from around here."

"Just get on the highway going eastbound. I'll tell you which exit." Mary Margaret called the realtor to arrange meeting her at the house. She was there waiting for them when they arrived.

"Oh, Marym, not a moment too soon. Is this Jason? Would you be a dear and hang them for me?"

"No and no. I don't touch the walls. But look at these for the boy's room." She looked at John. "Jason's only here for the labor." She showed off her work.

"Wow. That's incredible. It looks just like space. Not a hokey moon or planet in sight."

"Yeah. Jason had a great idea. Hang it on the ceiling, over his bed. It's like having a moon roof in your spaceship. This round one looks like a porthole."

Caitlin, the realtor, looked at the other large canvas. "This looks beautiful. It's going to make that fireplace pop. Oh, you always manage to make my houses look like they aren't all cookie cutter. They have personality. I could show five houses with same fireplace, but the one they'll ask about one with 'that fireplace with the painting.'"

Mary Margaret laughed. "You must be a hell of a salesman, because you show five houses and they're one of two floor plans. Do you want me to bill the office? Can you let me know what you think you'll need in the next couple of months? I'm bringing stuff to the Founder's Day show at Meadow Park and get rid of some inventory."

"I can do that. That's not for a few weeks. Do you mind if I stop over to your studio? I want to check out your inventory before you sell it out from under me."

"Can do. Let me know when you want to meet me there."

"Is it possible for Jason to put the one for the other house in my car?"

66

Mary Margaret looked at John. "It is possible? Yes, if Jason's bad back isn't bothering him. Jason?"

"I don't mind. My back hasn't bothered me in a while." He took the painting and transferred it to the realtor's car. "All set," he said.

"Thank you, Jason." Caitlin said and looked at her watch. "I've gotta run. Nice to see you. Marym, these are exactly what I needed. You never disappoint. Bye." She got in her car and left.

John pulled the keys to the truck out of his pocket and jingled them. "You want these back?"

"Not really. You sick of driving?"

"Not at all. Do you want to go home? Coffee? Drink?"

"I think I'd like a glass of wine. I rarely drink, but I'm in the mood. Do you know someplace with a patio or a deck? I'd like to sit outside."

"Off the top of my head, the golf course. Do you have any ideas?"

"The golf course sounds good to me." It was a short drive, but when he pulled in the parking lot he drove around a bit looking for a parking spot. Mary Margaret laughed at him.

"I know what you're doing. You're driving around so all the men can admire you in the truck. You're such a guy."

"That's right," he said, copping to his vanity. He parked in the next spot he found that fit the truck.

They walked in the restaurant to see about a table outside. He was on a first name basis with the hostess, and it seemed he knew everyone in the place. It took a minute to get outside; every few feet someone wanted to say hello or talk to him. Mary Margaret knew a number of the same people. Many of them expressed surprise seeing her there. A couple of people asked her if she took up golf.

John took her by the hand and pulled her to the door. The hostess waited patiently for them. She pointed to a table in the shade. "You'll fry out here otherwise," was her advice. She ushered them over and once seated gave them a menu. John took Mary Margaret's hand. It felt nice and warm, and it gave her little tingles that crept up her arm. He didn't let go of her hand until he held the chair out to seat her. Mary Margaret missed the feeling of his touch. As soon as they sat a waitress came over and took their drink order.

"Hi John," the waitress said. "Oh, hey Marym, how are you? I didn't know you golfed."

"Hi Hannah. I don't golf. I just drink."

"Your drinks will be right out. In the meantime, have you looked at the menu?"

"Let's have the appetizer sampler," John said, and looked at Mary Margaret. She nodded yes. "You shouldn't drink on an empty stomach." Someone else he knew served them their drinks. It was finally just the two of them. They looked at each other, both of them smiling. "Where to start?" He asked her.

"You go first. I imagine you have more questions than I do," she said, sipping her wine.

"You sure? I'm scared the first thing out of my mouth you'll get up and say, 'that's it!'; stab me with a knife, and game over." He said and sipped his beer.

"Stab you with a knife? Come on, it's a butter knife."

"All the more painful." He sat back and looked at her, an unreadable expression on his face. "Alright. This should be innocuous enough. Who is Jason?"

"Jason? He's the kid that cuts my lawn. I also hire him to do odd jobs. He's a starving artist who lives in his parent's basement. I give him space in my studio for free. He's supposed to help me do the labor-intensive stuff like moving things. Some of the larger canvases need two people to move the paint around, so he helps with that. He keeps the studio clean. When it's my month to run the meeting, he helps with that, too. I hope you don't mind I called you Jason. That dope of a realtor's met him about fifty times. She knew you weren't him. I didn't tell her your name because she's only going to forget it."

"What's the monthly meeting?"

"The Warehouse is run like a hippie's dream. Each month we have a meeting in the theater. We rotate studios so everyone has to take a turn. There's a box by the freight elevator that people put things they want addressed. At the meeting, we go over it. One person a year is the treasurer, and there's also a co treasurer to keep them honest. They collect the rent, handle the budget. The money is used for upkeep in the studio space and utilities.

"The bottom floor manages themselves unless it's a structural issue. There's a general manager that oversees use of the free spaces. Like if a kid made a movie and wants to use the theater to premiere it, the manager decides if it's acceptable. If it's inflammatory or porn, then no. If a band wants to book a show and use the stage, the GM decides if it's acceptable. If it's gang-related or white supremacists, no. It's supposed to be where kids can go and freely express themselves, without fear. Like rap battles and rap shows, nobody cares as long as the rules are followed.

"The GM, his name's Malik. He's cool and aware of the streets, so if there's the possibility of rivals showing up and trouble, he'll talk to whoever's running it to decide if they need a police presence or hire security. They can still hold their event, but they have to realize it's a multi-use place, and everyone's safety is the deciding factor. He gets a free studio for his trouble. The coffee house has open mic nights. The crowd runs from Birkenstock wearing granola heads to tattoos and Mohawks. It's painted over the entrance "All are welcome. This a place for You to do You. Leave everyone else alone."

"It sounds like a great idea. Quite an asset to the community."

"Yeah, like all great ideas it's doomed to fail."

"Wait a minute-Why?"

"Sooner or later, cultures will clash. The Urban versus the Suburban. Idealist versus realist. It's a shame. The intent is to encourage creativity and freedom of expression. You don't have to like it, or endorse it, or agree with it, but if Malik says it's cool, it's cool.

"I'm glad there's a place for the inner-city kids to go, to showcase their skills. All those kids hanging out on the corner because there's no alternative; that's a recipe for disaster." she sipped her wine and tucked a loose piece of hair behind her ear.

"If a kid expresses interest in something that's financially out of reach, like photography, Malik sees if one of the photographers would be willing to mentor the kid for a break on the rent. Or painting. I've had kids come up just see what I do. I mentored a couple of girls. Each girl got a chance to pour a canvas and take it home. Am I boring you?" she asked.

"No. Quite the opposite. It's an impressive way for cultures to mingle. A veritable societal subject experiment."

She nodded and continued. "Believe it or not, all any kid needs is a chance. If they get one and they don't take advantage of it, that's on them. But if they don't get a chance, that's on society. You can't save them all, but you shouldn't abandon them, either. I think things like this start out with the best of intentions, but they usually implode. They expand from the initial vision and get top heavy. You get people who want to use the success you created for their own gain."

"Why you little Marxist," John laughed. "Oh look. Our food's here." He pointed at her empty glass.

"Another round?" He didn't wait for answer and asked the server for two more. "Help yourself."

She speared a boneless wing and took a bite. "What's the rest of your summer look like?"

"No plans. You?" He said and grabbed a cheese stick.

"End of the month, I'm doing that Founder's Day thing in the park. Then two weeks in August, Summer Camp at the Warehouse."

"What's Summer Camp?"

"I'll tell you, but then I'm done talking. Summer Camp is a community event to combat boredom affecting kids in the neighborhood. The studios set up tents in the parking lot and invite everyone. They bring in basketball hoops, it's three on three. It starts between the cops and the firemen. Winner faces a challenger, usually three kids. Winner keeps playing until they lose. The winner faces another team. It keeps going."

"Jason and his friends build a half-pipe and skateboarders show off their skills. They try to get the kids interested in construction. It's funny how interested kids are in tools. They get to use a drill and stuff. The local sporting goods store donated kid-sized elbow and knee pads and helmets so the kids can try out skateboarding; to use what they just built. They take it apart each night to discourage after hours use, and the chance for interested kids to rebuild it each morning."

"A parent is supposed to sign them in and out, but sometimes it's a sibling. Last year, this ten-year-old girl came with her six-year-old brother, pushing a baby in a stroller. There was no adult around. She said they were home 'sleeping.' Usually, I get a couple older girls who hang around, and Jason's current love interest to help. One girl took the ten-year-old, and another, her brother. I watched the baby."

"After they played around with the paint, the girls took them around to check the other tents. The brother tried skateboarding. There was a tattooist. He tattooed his friends and gave the kids free fake tattoos. It runs from eleven until four. On Friday at four, there's a community cook out, the food donated. Sometimes the parents come with a dish to pass around and help."

"The little girl, her brother and the baby came every day. I watched the baby while she just got to be a kid for a while. Some of the moms came and watched, one of them said the ten-year-old got that rickety stroller out of the trash. They had the nerve to look down on this little girl who was all alone, doing a grown-up's job. That little girl deserved a gold star instead of mockery."

"I called Casey, asked her to go buy one and come down with a brand-new stroller. I knew the perception of white people coming in acting like saviors with their generosity, pat themselves on the back while they return to to their cushy house the suburbs; never to return again. Poverty is ongoing condition, and just because they're poor doesn't mean they don't deserve dignity."

"There's a huge trust issue between communities, and white people bearing gifts are suspect. Casey brought it with the excuse she already had one and didn't

71

need two. Her baby could only sit in one stroller at a time, so maybe somebody else could use it, and she left."

"Later, Jason came out with the stroller. He brought it over to the girl and said 'it was left out front. Why don't you take it before someone else does.' It allowed the girl to accept something without being accused of taking charity from white folks. You have to be careful of the culture. The little girl was elated, her brother mad because he get didn't anything. The thing is someone with no stroller will steal it from her. I bet it's gone by the end of the summer. What's even sadder, a family member might steal it and sell it for drug money. Even though that's the reality, it's still no reason not to try."

"It sounds like if you're not from the neighborhood, you're not welcome. That's a big hurdle any do-gooder not sensitive to the environment has to surmount." John said.

"That's true. Those rich white suburbanites have no clue. They show up at Christmas with food and gifts and feel great about themselves, but where are they the other 364 days of the year? People are hungry in the summer, too. We try. Malik has a couple coolers we all stock with peanut butter and jelly sandwiches, juice boxes and fruit. The sign doesn't say 'free lunch.' It says 'Hungry? Take a sandwich.' The women who run the coffee shop are from the community, and the coolers are kept inside the door there because the first time we tried it we left the coolers outside, and somebody stole them. Are you sure I'm not boring you?" Mary Margaret asked.

John shook his head no. "Quite the opposite."

"Anyway, Summer Camp is our way of getting accepted by the community. It's a lot of fun. Last year there were two girls who had issues with each other. I don't know what they were, I didn't really care. In Fluid Art, the more successful you are at tilting, the better the outcome."

"So, I got out two big canvases and had each girl put paint down on half, and each took their end and started tilting. The point being they had to work together for the best result. If one got really aggressive, it was her side that suffered. That was pretty interesting. They worked well together. They finished and started fighting who got to keep which canvas. I told them neither of them chose which canvas they got to keep, so they had to good job on both. When they were done, they invited a guy from out front. He officiated. They played 'Rock-paper-scissors three times. Best two out of three chose first."

"The last day we don't pour. We put their art up all over place and they have to find their canvas and take it home. Since it's supposed to be a family barbecue that last day, we primarily set up what they accomplished at camp to showcase their achievements to any adults they bring."

"We found this couple that ran an inner-city restaurant. They wanted to be involved. They brought this big barbecue smoker. Wegman's donated hot dogs and burgers. They cooked them and had other ethnic cuisine. Jason and his friends tried collard greens. Kids got to play ball."

"They skateboarded. They found the photos they took of each other. The paintings. The clay sculptures. We even had plywood boards and spray paint. They taught us how to graffiti. It was great fun and an even greater photo op. Last year was the first time. I hope we have the same success this year. I think about the little girl with her brother and the baby. If she shows up, she'll probably have two babies. She's probably moved. Who knows?"

"For being mean you have an altruistic streak a mile wide," John said. "I think that old cantankerous coot display is just a smokescreen. You actually have a heart in there somewhere, under lock and key for safekeeping. It's interesting. A lot of women your age play bridge or take up golf, and here you are, trying to save the world."

Mary Margaret's eyebrows furrowed her brow and said, "Women my age?"

John laughed. "Okay, women my age."

Mary Margaret narrowed her eyes. "Thank you, I think. I think of it as participating in a great big social experiment. Does an investment like this pay off? Do the Arts matter to the community? Do they provide enough value to keep investing in them? Can you take an us versus them mentality and create we? We'll see. It's a lot of work and exhausting, so it better be worth the effort." Their glasses empty and appetizers were finished. "Wow. I've been talking for hours. I'm done."

Their server approached and offered to clear their table and if they wanted anything else. John ordered another round.

"Really? Another drink? I'm not sure I can handle three."

"You talked through the first two. Have one, sit back and enjoy it. Even though I have a lot more questions I promise I won't ask them."

"Like what?"

"Like I'm not even sure what's your last name. You told me it was Welch. You told someone else, Miller." He said as the server dropped off their drinks.

"Good. I'm not telling. I haven't had that many to start revealing personal details." She sat back and looked around. The place was busy, the tables turned over quickly, but nobody bothered them. It was a gorgeous summer day, even though it was hot, and the sun beat down, they were in the shade. A slight breeze blew just enough to make it comfortable. The springy curls that formed around her hairline floated in the breeze. They sat there in silence and enjoyed their drinks. It wasn't too long before someone approached them. It was his friend Dr. Stewart.

"Hello John, former patient of mine." He said, nodding at Mary Margaret.

"It's Mary Margaret," she said. He took her chin and moved her face to better see her injury.

"Very nice. It's a little red, but in six months you won't be able to see it. You never came back to get the stitches out. Whoever did it did a good job."

"My daughter, Casey. She's an RN."

"Casey? Does she work at the hospital? Pretty girl who looks like you?"

Mary Margaret nodded; her face turned red. "Some people think so."

She sat quietly while he and John talked about golf and old friends. They golfed in a league and there was much talk about that; Mary Margaret tuned them out and thought about Casey. She was such a good person. She worked too much and going to school placed too much stress on her, but she was young and pursuing her dreams. *A mother can't not worry,* she thought.

"Hey, Mary Margaret, where'd you go?" John said to her.

"Sorry, just daydreaming."

"About me?"

"What? No." She hesitated. "What if I was?"

"That would make me very happy. I enjoy you, and your complicated life. I've never met anyone so interesting." John smiled at her. She smiled back.

"I think you've confused me with a social justice warrior. I'm just an artist with a plan."

"A plan? It's way bigger than that. Here you are. A beautiful woman with an old soul trying to save the world, or at least your corner of it."

Mary Margaret was stuck on the word beautiful. *Did he really say that about me?* She felt her neck grow warm and her face flushed. *He can't be serious. Women my age have a certain attractiveness but aren't beautiful.*

"I think it's time to go. We've monopolized this table long enough." He settled the tab without accepting any money from her. When he reached out his hand for hers, she let him take it. They walked that way back to her truck. They got in, and he drove it to her house. He offered to walk Stella.

"Look at her, waiting in the window. Probably dying for a walk." John said.

"Sorry. That bone's in the yard. The bone."

"She can have it after her walk," he told her.

"You know, I'm in the mood for a walk myself. Mind if I come with?"

"It's fine with me, but you better check with Stella."

Stella was very excited. About the bone. She ran right passed them and ran right over to it.

75

"See. Told you."

John went inside and got her leash. Stella wasn't happy to be separated from the bone but forgot about it by they reached the corner. He took Mary Margaret's hand to help her cross the street; once on the other side he continued to hold her hand and she didn't pull it away. By the time they'd reached the park, it was early evening.

It was the perfect time to walk in the park, the joggers and kids home for dinner. They walked in silence. He liked holding her hand and wasn't going to open his mouth and ruin it. He'd never speak again if it meant they could live suspended in time in this exact moment. He blinked a few times to get that thought out of his head and said to her, "What?"

"What's what?"

"What's on your mind? You haven't asked me anything all day. Isn't there anything you want to know about me? My feelings are hurt you don't want to know any details."

"What do I want to know? Huh. Let me think. OK. How about this. I have one daughter, an adult, but she lives here. Five minutes away. What's it like to have to actually make plans to see your kids?"

"You couldn't start with anything easier?" He laughed. "My sons. When we were a family and still lived in Philly, they were always home for the holidays. We would leave after Christmas and spend the New Year in Vermont skiing with my brother and his family. We did that for years, but the boys started to want to spend New Years Eve with their friends, so we stayed home. As they got college-aged, it was even more fractured."

"I think without those traditions, the cracks in my marriage became obvious. What was more obvious we passed craters into voids. With the boys gone, we needed to reconnect with each other; but the only thing to she wanted to reconnect with was her lost youth. She underwent a huge transformation, you know about the boobs. But liposuction, and a facelift. Dyed her hair blonde, went to the gym. I wasn't concerned; all her friends did that."

"I traveled for work and didn't think about not being concerned until it was too late. She was out all the time. I worked and wanted to relax when I was home. I heard rumors about her social life, and guys. She would entertain at the house when I was on the road and the neighbors were more than happy to rat her out. I was willing to try to fix things, but she said I was too old." He rubbed his forehead as if the memory still stung.

"That was bad, but when it slipped out she was entertaining; she was entertaining in our bed. When I thought about some other guy on my side of the bed, his head on my pillow, I realized my marriage was over. I packed a bag and checked into a hotel. They boys were moving around, so it was easier for me to meet up with them. It didn't revolve around a holiday, it was more logistics."

"My oldest, graduated law school and settled in D.C. He got sick about ten years ago, with leukemia. He's fine now, he had a successful bone marrow transplant. I get there and all his skeletons fall out of the closet. He's gay, and his partner's name was Jeff. He never said anything because he thought I'd disapprove of his lifestyle. I don't know how I would have felt if circumstances were different. I couldn't think about that. He was dying. My son was going to die. Jeff was there every second of it; he was there through the worst of it when no family was there to help."

"In a gift from God, it was a one in a million chance, but my other son was a perfect match. Brian was cured, and because of Jeff being with him he was never alone. He had a slow recovery and Jeff nursed him back to health. Compare having your kid gay and alive, or straight and dead. Alive wins. His sex life is his business. I don't care."

"My other son, Peter lives outside of Dallas. He's married to a wonderful girl, Sarah, and they have a daughter, Callie. Or Carol. I'm not sure if she started school yet. Peter has custody of my ex-wife. Whenever there is a family function, Peter's always the host, his wife does a wonderful job. Jeff is really good at managing Kathy, my ex."

"If she starts drinking, she starts feeling sorry for herself, it always dissolves into a 'poor me' session, but damn, Jeff can talk her off the ledge and distract her with something else. The guy should be a hostage negotiator. My wife cannot accept the fact she got old. She can lift, tighten and fill; but she's still old. After almost losing my son, old is good. I'll take every day God gives me and be grateful for the opportunity."

"Kathy can't look at it that way, so I'm glad we're divorced. I look at her now and think 'what a drag she turned out to be.'" He looked down at their hands, still entwined. He looked at her. She grabbed her hand back, the spell broken.

"Sorry. I forgot we were holding hands." Mary Margaret said.

"I'm not."

She deliberately let that remark go over her head. Mary Margaret had too much of a buzz to figure out exactly what was so wrong with him holding her hand. Nothing as far as she could tell. It felt nice. It was warm and dry; no sweaty palms to turn her off. He let go gracefully and allowed her to retreat with dignity. He held Stella's leash, and they continued their walk, mostly in quiet. They came back around to the entrance and waited for the light to change.

When it did, he grabbed her hand again and helped her cross the street. Once on the other side he let go without her asking. She couldn't understand why it bothered her he had done so. After all, that's what she wanted. *Wasn't it?* She asked herself. *Geez, remind me never to drink during the day.* It wasn't too much later when they arrived back at her house. As soon as she was unclipped, Stella bolted for the bone. They leaned against her truck and watched Stella go to town on that bone. "Thank you for the bone. That elevated you to most favored guest to Stella."

"Screw Stella. What do I have to do to be elevated in your eyes?" John asked her.

"I'm sorry, John. I can't answer that. I wish I knew. It's been so long flying solo I don't know if I'll ever be comfortable enough to give up the controls."

"You don't have to give them up, you know. You could maybe share them."

"I think I've only ever trusted two men in my life. My dad and Ben. I said good-bye to my dad one morning when I was in tenth grade. He had a heart attack and died. I never saw him again. And Ben, things were great until he fell in love with someone else. I just think it's better this way. I have terrible instincts when it comes to relationships. If you're a normal, reasonable guy, go find someone healthy. You'll be better off."

"In case you weren't listening, my ex-wife said I was old. I might be normal and reasonable, but I'm old."

"Why does that matter?"

"Exactly. It doesn't matter at all. My point is she could have said I was a cheater, a drunk, a wife beater, a lot of good reasons to leave your husband. But because I was old? She wasn't that far behind me. I'll admit it messed with my head for a couple of years. I mean, who'd be interested in me? I'm old. Who'd want me? I'm old."

"Maybe on the outside. I can't help that. But I'm not dead. It all came down to the fact that my son, my young son almost died. I could say, 'I'm old. Get me a rocking chair and the remote, and leave whatever's left on the table, but I decided no. So, what I'm old? I'm also a lot of other things, good things that have value. I know what it's like to feel rejected because of who you are, something you can't do anything about. It cuts deep and leaves scars." He looked at her to see if it touched a nerve; if she had any scars she wanted to keep hidden.

"Old? You're not even that old." She said, no comment about her scars forthcoming.

"See? Not to you. I shouldn't have let my wife mindfuck me as much as she did. I wasted a lot of time believing she was right. I took a job in California to get as far as possible away from her. I went to the land of endless sunshine and eternal youth to convince myself I was't too old. If that isn't counterintuitive, I don't know what is; but I realized people get old in California, too. They celebrate life anyway. I'm middle aged in California. I should have stayed there. Yes, if you want to feel old, you'll get old."

"I finally figured out getting old was her problem, not mine. She was old. She was doing everything possible to avoid getting old. I reminded her she was getting old, so fucking all these younger guys proved otherwise. She was so stupid. Guys fucked her because guys will pretty much fuck anything."

"I decided I was getting older, but I was not old yet. Age is just a number. Cliche, but true. Once I wrapped my head around that and forgave myself for falling into that trap, I moved on. Maybe you should forgive yourself for whatever you've been carrying around that's preventing you from enjoying the rest of your life."

Her eyes looked off to the side as if reliving a painful memory when she said "My shit's buried so deep it would probably take a shrink twenty years to get to the bottom of it. I'd be dead by then. Besides, I don't feel like I'm missing anything. I'm doing exactly what I want when I want to do it, and I there's nobody to tell me otherwise. That's the way I like it."

"If that's the way you want it, fine, but I can't see how that makes you happy. When was the last time anybody hugged you? Kissed you? Let you lean on them when you feel down?" He looked at her. "You don't have to answer. It doesn't matter. If you're happy, there's no need for anything more."

"What's the point of all this?" Mary Margaret asked. "Why are you stirring all this shit up? You don't even live here. I'm supposed to get all emotional over some guy who is just going to leave. No thanks. I'm not looking for permanent. I don't do temporary. It's been so long since I've done anything I think all the rules have changed, so why bother? Am I supposed to throw myself at you? Or make you earn it? I have no clue."

"This: practically throw yourself at me, so I know you're into me, and give me the chance to earn the rest. It's not going to happen unless you say so."

"Oh, I say so."

"You say so?

"I say it's so not gonna happen."

He let her push him away. "I think it's time I go. Thanks for showing me the Warehouse. It was fun." John walked over and got in his car. He gave a little wave as he drove off.

***

80

Mary Margaret didn't talk to him for a couple of weeks. She missed him, surprisingly. So many things occupied her day. It broke up missing him into manageable chunks, until the end of the day when she totaled up the time. It was quite a bit more than she thought.

Mary Margaret swore she'd never be involved with another man after Dan. He hurt her in ways she couldn't talk about. But John seemed to be a genuinely nice guy. He had some miles on him as well, but so what? *Don't do it,* she told herself. *Don't fall for some guy who already had an exit plan. You'll only get hurt again.* She felt like a light switch that hadn't been turned on in years only to have John come along and with a flick of his finger light her up like a teenage girl. *This can't be happening. I can't have feelings for, I don't want feelings for him. But I do. Shit.*

He thought about her, too, only over long expanses of time. John didn't know what he wanted. Mary Margaret was right. He would be leaving. Maybe not right away, but soon. Soonish. John didn't understand why a woman as incredible as she hadn't been scooped up. Were the men in this town so stupid they couldn't see what a treasure she was? Was she socially deficit in some way he hadn't yet seen? John stayed away from her on purpose.

Maybe she knew something he didn't. Her lack of excitement at his approach hurt him. So, she wasn't into him. No law said she had to be. But he didn't believe it. He liked her. That afternoon, they had a nice time. She let him hold her hand. Then she put him on ice. He didn't think Patton ever thought so much about a campaign. He avoided her because he lost ground every time he saw her, and soon he'd owe her ground.

***

Chapter Six

Founder's Day was another marketing attempt by the local suburban officials to create a sense of community. A parade, a farmer's market, craft fair, sidewalk sales along Main Street, family friendly activities, for the teens a battle of the bands in the park. A chicken barbeque capped off by fireworks. Friday night was set up, Saturday the event, ending with the fireworks. They used to make it last the weekend, but by Sunday interest fizzled out. So, one jam packed Saturday, the last Saturday in July was set aside in the pursuit or illusion of community pride and joy.

It happened innocently enough at work. They were reworking the cables in Westbrook Hall, and John spent most of the day crawling around looking for outlets and connections. It was hard to focus, he hadn't seen Mary Margaret in a few weeks. Instead of decreasing the amount of time he spent thinking about her, he thought about her more. Thinking about her more annoyed him, and the inability to stop thinking about her pissed him off to no end.

Evelynne, his university contact for Westbrook Hall, was talking about Founders Day while he worked. He mostly nodded and said uh-huh. She talked it up quite a bit so when she suggested he go as her guest and really get a feel of being a local, he nodded his head and uh-huh-ed one too many times.

When he first moved to town, John went out with Evelynne. He met her at work. She was cute, divorced, and easy to be around. He did more than go out with her, they had a fling. He was a normal, healthy male and her interest in him was flattering. They dated and went out for about six months. She was great in the sack; an open and a willing participant.

One night found them talking about the future in her bed, blanketed by the afterglow of lovemaking. Evelynne cuddled up next to him under the sheets, naked. He found himself distracted by the smoothness of her skin.

Whenever he tried to talk about his version of their future, she would hump his leg and remind him of what was on the table. John like her, enjoyed spending time with her, and had fun with her. She was a hell of a good time. He waffled whenever she brought up the future, which was more often in the last few weeks. Evelynne wanted the promise of a future with him, starting with being exclusive and not seeing other people. John balked at that. He didn't know enough people there to make a pledge of fidelity, and he found her rush for him to do disconcerting. The more she pushed, the less he wanted to give. Evelynne finally gave him an ultimatum. Be boyfriend and girlfriend or else.

John opted for the 'or else,' explaining that the transient nature of his job meant months would go by without seeing her, and it wasn't going to work. She tried to reframe everything so the pieces would fit, but his answer was still no. He was never going to be more than a casual fling, and since they wanted different things, they should end it before she hated him for not delivering what she wanted.

That's the way they left it. John spoke to her often about the job, but not much else. They remained friends although he was very careful around her. He got the feeling she was waiting him out to realize she was the best thing in town, and then in a moment of weakness swoop in and lock him down.

John found himself agreeing to meet her by the fountain in the square at two o'clock. He immediately felt like he was cheating on Mary Margaret, but decided a woman who had no interest in him didn't deserve his loyalty. Maybe his male ego got the best of him, but John would go, and he would have fun with Evelynne whether it made him miserable or not. John just had to be certain he didn't send her the message there was an opening for the more she hoped to get from him.

*** *** ***

Chapter Seven

Founder's Day was named after some revolutionary war hero nobody knew. James T. Harper served with George Washington. He crossed the Potomac River with him and is one of the men immortalized in the famous painting. When the war ended, he settled here and established Harpersville. A single man, he never married and died within less than a year. Over the next hundred years it changed names a couple of times, only to have some eight-grader do a research project; and discovered the history of J.T. Harper and original name of the town. The boy initiated a drive to have it returned to honor their fallen soldier.

There was an old cemetery in the middle of a farmer's field. The farmers family went back generations, and nobody ever knocked it down and plowed it under out of respect for their ancestors. Exposure to the elements over the years polished the stones smooth and most of them were unreadable, except for a few. A girl in the same eighth-grade class was doing for her history project how many generations her family, the farmers, had lived there and if there were any uncovered historical gems. She went out in the field and did gravestone rubbings, hoping she would discover something that made her family interesting and not just a bunch of old farmers. One of the few readable rubbings disclosed the final resting place of J.T. Harper; some miles away from the center of town.

Because his parents probably wanted this to appear on a college entrance application, they supported his drive to restore the original name. There was a groundswell of approval, but no money available to make it happen. The best they could do was come up with enough money to pay for a brass plaque and place it by the fountain in the center of town, embedded in stone donated by the Memories in Stone monument company. It became known as Founder's Square, an integral part of what created Founder's Day.

Jason was around to help Mary Margaret set up her tent in the ten' x ten' square allotted to her. Upfront was a table and two chairs. She brought four big pieces and displayed them leaning against the table to create interest in her goods. Behind her were different sized smaller paintings. She sat up front and chatted up the people who stopped by; Jason worked behind her to help people chose from the display.

If something wasn't exactly right, he searched the inventory for what might work. She priced her things by size. If someone expressed a specific desire for something size or color related, she usually came away with a commissioned piece. She also kept a cooler full of bottled water on ice she sold for a buck. She only did that because people kept asking her if she knew where they could get a drink; it was hot under those tents if no breeze blew. Jason was in charge of that too, and got to keep any profits.

Since Founder's Day was primarily a family event, after less than an hour John had seen enough and was ready to go. Evelynne, however, wanted to show him Founder's Day in its entirety. She motivated him to go to the park and look at all the crafter tables with the promise of food. As they wandered around and looked at things, she stayed tight against him and pulled on his hand when she found something of interest.

Evelynne dragged him over to look at a booth featuring macrame goods made by a husband and his wife. John thought they looked like pair of retired bookkeepers. Evelynn was so excited to see macrame, she looked over every wall or plant hanger on display. He looked around at the jewelry makers and woodworkers, they all seemed to run together after a while. John noticed across the way a large, colorful canvas propped up against a table. That must be Mary Margaret's booth. He saw a tall, skinny kid with long hair, that must be Jason. He didn't see her and was secretly glad. He didn't know how to explain Evelynne and why was she hanging off him. John doubted she'd even be interested in an explanation.

"Look, John! See this wall hanging? Wouldn't it go perfectly over the couch?"

He looked at the looped and knotted rope hanging off a wooden dowel. It was a macrame owl.

"Yes," he said, despite his personal opinion it was hideous. She purchased it and squealed with delight. Evelynne hugged his arm with pleasure, thinking someday in the future they would be having coffee and she would point to it and say, 'Remember, John, when we bought that? At the Founder's Day craft fair?'

John could feel her touching him, moving closer at every opportunity. He didn't feel like confronting her about it. He wasn't leading her on, she was leading herself on. There was nothing he could do about it now anyway, so he chose to ignore it.

They meandered around, looking at different things. He tried to steer her away from Mary Margaret's booth. Evelynne was more than happy to let John lead her around, that meant he was having a good time with her. He thought he was successful in avoiding Mary Margaret's booth.

Like most craft shows, one aisle looked the same as another and he got turned around. What he thought was the exit landed him in front of the booth with the colorful display of Mary Margaret's art. John was glad Mary Margaret wasn't there. He wanted to take his time and look at her work. Evelynne hung off his arm, not impressed. "Come on, John," and pulled at him.

The guy he presumed as Jason came over to see if he could help them. John selected a larger canvas and said "This right here, Evelynne. This would look perfect over the couch."

"You think?" She said in a pouty voice. "It looks like somebody vomited in technicolor, like someone puked up a garden."

"Hey, double M." Jason called to the girl on her hands and knees off to the side, who up to this point went unnoticed by John. She was down there sorting canvases. "This lady said it looked like someone puked all over the canvas." The girl sat back on her heels.

"Help me up, Jason," the girl said. It was no girl, it was Mary Margaret. She got to her feet and looked at John, carrying Evelynne's purchases while she dangled off his arm. She made no indication she recognized him. "Yes, it takes something special to hang over your couch. If it looks like vomit, it might not be the right piece for you."

Evelynne took one of the bags from John and removed the macrame owl wall hanging. She held it up for them to admire. "See, something like this would be perfect, wouldn't it, John?" and hugged him closer. He remained silent, unsure what to do.

"It's lovely," Mary Margaret said, "if you like knots that look like they were tied by a drunken sailor." Evelynne smiled, unsure if she had just been insulted.

John pointed to one of the large canvases. "I'd like to buy that one."

"Oh, I'm sorry. That one's sold."

He selected another. "That one."

"Sold."

"This one."

"Unavailable. Don't waste your time. Everything here is *unavailable*."

John took a step back and looked at Mary Margaret. Now, she looked like an artist. Her hair was in a messy pile on top her head, she wore a flannel shirt splattered with paint with the sleeves cut off. She had on black gym shorts and work boots with tube socks crushed around her ankles. John tried to catch her eye, but she wouldn't look at him. Jason and Evelynne detected the tension between them; because of this, Evelynne dug in and stepped next to John, wedging herself under John's arm as if in an embrace.

"Come on, baby." She said, "You've been such a good sport taking me shopping. Let's go find you something to eat."

"Yes, baby." Mary Margaret said. "There's a food truck round-up over in the municipal lot if you can't wait for the chicken barbeque." She watched as Evelynne turned him around and pulled John off in the direction of the street.

Once they exited the park, Evelynne said. "That girl is weird. Seriously weird."

"What girl?" John asked.

"Her. The painter. Mary Margaret. Oh, that's right, you're not from around here. Trust me, stay away from her. She's as nutty as they come."

But I like nuts, he thought. *The saltier, the better.*

Over at her tent, Jason was thoroughly confused. What was the deal with Mary Margaret? He'd never seen her so aggravated by a customer.

"What was that all about?" Jason asked her. "Why wouldn't you sell him something?"

"My stuff does not belong hung next to some piece of shit macrame wall hanging. Or even hung in the same house." Mary Margaret said spitefully.

"Well, you just missed out on a hundred bucks and that's one more canvas I have to lug back home."

"Shut up, Jason."

After they ate John wanted to leave. Evelynne wanted to stay for the fireworks. John calculated in his head how much longer they had until dark and it much longer than he wanted to spend with her. What he really wanted to do was fuck her brains out and rub Mary Margaret's nose in it. A bell went off in his brain, signaling that if he started things back up with Evelynne, he'd never get rid of her. He tried to disengage his arm but once in her possession she wasn't giving it back.

Mary Margaret fumed at the sight of John with Evelynne. She didn't know why the sight of them together pissed her off. Mary Margaret had a chance with John, but she turned him down without giving him a shot. She wondered if they were still friends. Mary Margaret wasn't even sure if they were friends. Was he even enough of a friend to be considered banished to the Friend Zone?

What was he doing with her picking out something to place over Evelynne's couch? If she sold him a painting and he hung it over that dipshit Evelynne's couch, would he think of her every time he walked into Evelynne's living room? After he left for good, she could see Evelynne's first move to throw the painting in the trash. *That was the problem*, she thought. *I know I'm not Rembrandt, and it wasn't meant to a part of a person's permanent collection, but still, I created it.*

If someone got rid of a piece because it didn't match a new decor scheme, so be it. If you pitch it the garbage because the artist wouldn't share a swing with you in second grade, no. Absolutely not.

"What's wrong, double M?" Jason asked her. "Are you crushing on some guy who already has a girlfriend?"

"What? No. It was that woman. I went to school with her. She was one of a group of girls who were popular and bitches to those of us who weren't."

"You're lying." Jason called her on it. "I bet when you were in school you didn't care if you were popular. You're that lone wolf who went her own way and probably didn't even know who was popular. It's the guy. He wanted your attention and you wouldn't even look at him. Why not?"

"I guess he did hit on me, and I shot him down."

"Yeah, but why did you do that if you like him?"

"Who said I liked him?"

"You did. Body language. If you didn't like him, you would have sold him whatever he wanted, took the dude's money and laughed all the way to the bank. Instead, you avoid looking at him. You had a frown on your face the whole time. I bet you're still thinking about him, and it's agitated you. Why'd you treat him like that?"

"Because I'm a lone wolf. Getting involved with him would only slow me down."

"Even a lone wolf likes to have fun once in a while."

"He's only here temporarily. There's no point in pursuing what's over before it even begins."

"That makes no sense. If you're not interested in him long term, that's perfect. You don't have to dump him when you get sick of him. He's already on his way out."

"Shut up, Jason. You can't even remember your girlfriend's name."

"I know. That's why I call them all 'babe.'"

The discussion ended when a young couple approached their booth. They were getting married and decorating on a budget. They were very interested in the larger canvases. They wanted to compare them all laid out so they could decide. The table was wide enough to accommodate the two large paintings already leaning against it, so Mary Margaret and Jason each took the two on the end and leaned them against their knees; all four now displayed in a row for evaluation. The couple went back and forth, unable to make up their minds. A hundred dollars was an awful lot for them, they didn't want to waste it. The girl was torn between two of them, the guy so in love with her he wanted whatever made her happy.

Since the one against Mary Margaret's legs was out of the running, she placed it back in its original spot and went to the back of the tent. She sorted through the smaller pieces until she found the one she was looking for; it complemented the one the woman was leaning towards. She passed the one she held to the guy.

"Here's what we can do," she said to the couple. "You like that one, right? I found a smaller matching piece. If you buy the bigger one, I'll bring the price down to seventy-five and throw in the little one as a wedding gift."

"You would do that?" The girl asked.

"For you, sure."

"Oh, Ryan! Let's do it!" He got out his wallet and paid Jason while Mary Margaret wrapped up the smaller item. She passed it forward as Jason put the large painting in one of these thin, extra, extra-large plastic garbage bags.

"Here you go," Mary Margaret said and smiled. "Congratulations on your upcoming wedding." She watched the happy couple walk away. A gentleman who watched the exchange came over. He pointed to the one they didn't choose.

"Make me the same offer and I'll by this one." He said.

"I'd love to, but I'm a starving artist and can't give away the store. What I can do is either /or. Either get the big one for seventy-five dollars or pay full price and get a free one."

"Do I get to choose the free one?" He countered.

"As long as it's not bigger than 11x14." He moved inside the tent and went through her inventory. He chose one. "This one?"

"Yes. Pay full price and you can get that one for free."

"Deal," he said, and pointed at the larger canvas he selected. "Wrap them up."

After he left Mary Margaret gave Jason the hundred-dollar bill. "Here," she said. "Gas money."

"That dude must have really gotten under your skin if you're giving money away." She looked at him. "I know," he said. "Shut up, Jason."

John couldn't talk Evelynne into going home, but there was nothing else that interested him besides Mary Margaret, and interested wasn't what he was. He was angry. She was so mean to him. She made it plain he wasn't a candidate for her affection. That was fine. Mary Margaret made that absolutely clear. Evelynne interrupted his thoughts.

"John," she teased. "Let's go do something."

"I know," he said. "Why don't we get some ice cream?" He figured she couldn't talk with an ice cream cone in her mouth. Her voice grated on him. She managed to take his one syllable name into a whole sentence. 'Jooooooohhhhhhhnnnnnn.' He got them both large cones and they sat on the stone wall that reinforced the fountain. John figured a large cone would shut her up for a while and leave him to his thoughts. His thoughts. What was it? Mary Margaret, of course.

John returned to her behavior at her booth. She was openly hostile; she wouldn't sell him a painting. Granted, she did overhear Evelynne compare her work to vomit. If she was mad about that, he could understand, but he shouldn't be mad at him; she should be mad at Evelynne. She was the one who said it.

John wanted to buy a painting, but Mary Margaret refused to sell him anything. She wouldn't even look him in the eye. Evelynne said she was weird. Maybe there was bad blood between them, and she was mad he brought her around. She might be mad he brought her. She might be mad he was with another woman.

Could Mary Margaret be jealous? A lightbulb went off over his head. That was possible. Casey said she was a cream puff. Perhaps her feelings were hurt, and instead of hurt she responded with anger. John mulled that over for a while until Evelynne finished her cone.

"John," Evelynne said, after she finished, "let's go check out the band. They're playing oldies."

The craft fair was ending; the vendors breaking down their displays and packing up their wares. While she sorted the paintings into the appropriate boxes, she sent Jason for the dolly. She was on her hands and knees when a voice behind her said, "I'll buy them all!"

"Casey! How are you? You managed to get a weekend off?" Mary Margaret said, happy to see her daughter dressed in anything other than scrubs. She scrambled to her feet.

"I've decided to put the brakes on the overtime, at least until Labor Day. Life's too short."

"I'm almost done. Oh look, it's Jason. Jason, if I give you the key to my truck can you finish loading it up and take everything back to my house? Just park it all in the garage. Leave the truck. Your car is parked there, I can get a ride from somebody else. I'd like to spend a sometime with Casey."

"Hi, Jason." Casey greeted him.

"Hello, um, Casey," he said back. He could feel his face turn bright red and felt the back of his neck grow warm. She was a couple years older and Jason had been infatuated with her since he was a freshman in high school, she a senior. "Yes, double M, I can do that, it's no big deal."

"Thank you, Jase. I didn't even ask you, Casey, if you had any time to spend. Do you have plans? Do you have time to grab a bite to eat? I'm starving."

"Yes, I do. I was hoping to catch up with you, it's been so long."

"Do you need anything else, Jason? I've got my phone if you need me."

"It's all good. Have fun. Goodbye, Casey."

"Goodbye, Jason." Casey said.

They walked over to the municipal lot, stopping frequently to say hello to people they haven't seen since last year's Founder's Day. It was a beautiful summer day and the place was crawling with people. They came to watch the fireworks which weren't scheduled for a couple more hours, but people put their chairs down to reserve a spot. Some people sat and read while their children ran around, others wandered around talking to old friends. The dinner rush was over, the food trucks getting ready to pack it in, the smell from chicken barbecue wafted overhead. They both got the walk-away taco salads, piled high in a chips bag along with a bottle of water. They sat in the same place John and Evelynne did a few hours earlier.

"What brings you to Founder's Day, Casey? I imagine if I had a day off this is the last place I'd go."

"I'm meeting someone to watch the fireworks, but he doesn't get off 'til seven, and has go home and change."

"Interesting. 'He' doesn't get off until seven. Is he someone I know?"

"No. I met him at work. He's a doing a fellowship. This is the first night our schedules have met up with the same night off. What about you? How's your love life?"

"My love life? Nonexistent as usual. What made you bring that up?"

"That guy John. I saw him at the coffee shop. He asked about your eye. Have you seen him lately?"

"I saw him today. He was with his girlfriend."

"What girlfriend?"

"Evelynne Malzenski. They stopped by the booth. She was hanging all over him and she said my paintings looked like someone puked up a garden."

"Well, Mother, it is abstract art. It is subject to the viewer's interpretation."

"I'd be happier if she said it looked like a mortician threw up."

"Back to John. How is he?"

"He's dating that bitch Evelynne. I think he brought her by to rub my nose in it."

"Rub your nose in what?"

"That he's capable of having a healthy relationship and I'm not."

"Why would he think that?"

"Because I told him so."

"So you saw him before today and told him you were bad at love?"

"Yeah. I took him down to The Warehouse. We stopped for a drink, and one topic led to another. He was curious about my views as far adult romance, and I told him I didn't believe in it. I think he just wanted to drive the truck."

"Hold on. *Hold on.* You gave him your pin number, took him to your studio, had a drink, *and* let him drive your truck? Do you know the only other person you've brought downtown is me, and you had a drink with him plus he got to drive the truck? No wonder he thought you were interested."

"Well, he got over me quick. Besides, if you saw how tight he was with Evelynne, it looked like he was already seeing someone."

"Maybe you misunderstood. They could be just friends."

"She called him 'baby.' You don't call someone you just started seeing 'baby.'"

"Come on," Casey said, took the garbage and pitched it in a can. "I'm supposed to meet him at the entrance to the park. I'll introduce you." Casey gave her Mom the once over. "Maybe not. Mom, not to hurt your feelings, but you sort of look like a street person."

"You can get away with anything if you tell people you're an artist, Casey. They expect you to be eccentric."

"If you say so."

"I have really good teeth. Street people aren't religious about going to the dentist."

"Once again, if you say so." They stopped at the entrance to the park and waited. "Here he comes now, mom. Don't embarrass me."

A tall, dark-haired man approached them. He had as easy gait; comfortable in his skin. He was long and lean with very little body fat. He was dressed like an adult, no cargo pants or ball cap. He wore khaki chino shorts and a golf shirt, to his credit he didn't pop the collar. On his feet he wore a pair of broken-in Sperry topsiders. He dressed a lot like John, Mary Margaret observed. When he saw Casey his face split into a wide smile.

"Casey! Boy, you sure look different not wearing scrubs," he said and backtracked, "not that you don't look good in scrubs."

"I could say the same about you, Seth." Casey shot her mother a look. "Seth Greene, I'd like you to meet my mom, Mary Margaret Welch." When they divorced, Mary Margaret wanted to keep her married name while Casey was in school so they'd have the same last name. Ben and Sheila didn't mind. She never bothered to change it back, although she sometimes used Miller. That would mean she was the last Miller of her kind, too lonely even for her to contemplate.

"Pleased to meet you, Mrs. Welch." *His momma raised him right,* she thought.

"It's very nice to meet you, too. Please excuse my appearance. I'm a painter, and I had a booth today at the craft fair. There's no point in dressing well if you're going to be crawling around on your hands and knees looking for a particular painting."

"A painter? Is your work still up? I'd love to see it." Seth said.

"Unfortunately, it's over and taken down. Some other time, perhaps. Maybe Casey can bring you down to our Summer Camp. Enjoy the fireworks tonight. I'm heading out now."

"Mom, how are you going to get home? Jason took your truck."

"I'll walk. It's not too far. If I get tired, I'll call Jason. Seth, it was very nice to meet you. Casey, give your mom a kiss goodbye." Mary Margaret leaned towards her daughter and offered. her cheek. "She carries Mace and a switchblade in her purse." Mary Margaret said to Seth. "So, watch yourself."

"Please excuse my mother. She thinks she's funny. Time for you to leave, Mom. Maybe if I'm lucky you'll get kidnapped on your way home."

"One can always hope. Have a goodnight," Mary Margaret said and walked away, from the back she really did look like like a homeless person.

"Your mother is quite a character. Do you really have Mace in your bag?"

"Well, yeah. But only because she gave it to me for Christmas."

"Your Mom drives a truck?"

"She has one. A big, black, get-out-of-my-way truck."

"Cool." He said as he watched her walked away. He turned back to Casey and took her hand. "Now show me everything."

***

John was walking in endless circles with Evelynne, passing time until the fireworks. He was trying to figure out the best way to lose her. She wouldn't let go of his arm and kept rubbing up against him. To the casual observer they looked like a couple, and that irked him to no end.

They were not a couple and it irritated him other people would get the impression they were. She kept introducing him as 'my John.' They came across some of her friends and were asked if they wanted to join them to watch the fireworks. Something occurred to John; he asked Evelynne to step off to the side.

"Evelynne, I have to ask you a favor. I planned on staying for the fireworks, but I have to share something with you. I was in the Vietnam War. Fireworks sound too much like what I experienced, it takes me back and I suffer from PTSD. I've been through therapy and all, and I thought I was past it, but I can feel the anxiety rising and I'm getting nauseous. I'm afraid the fireworks will cause an episode of PTSD and flashbacks, the whole thing. Is it too much to ask you to watch them with your friends? Will you be able to find a ride home if I leave? I'm afraid I can't stay."

"Oh, John, how awful. Do you want me to come with you? Is there anything I can do?"

"No. I hate to ask you to stay alone, but I'm just going home to sit in the dark wearing ear plugs. That's no fun for you. I can feel the anxiety starting to build. I have to go now. I'm sorry but I've got to go NOW."

"John, take care of yourself. I can get a ride no problem, but I'm worried about you. I shouldn't leave you alone."

"Please, Evelynne, I know what I have to do. I have to go sit alone in the dark. Please try to understand. I'll make it up to you another time."

"Go, John, go. I understand." She said right before she pulled his head down and kissed him full on the lips.

John turned around and practically ran to his car. He couldn't get out of there fast enough.

John pulled out and quickly drove away from the park. He wouldn't put it past Evelynne to change her mind and chase after him. He passed by someone walking on the shoulder. *Geez*, he thought, *even small town U.S.A. Can't escape the homeless problem.* He glanced up, looking in the review mirror.

Holy Shit! That's Mary Margaret! He went through the light and turned around, only to have someone on his bumper make it impossible to slow down and talk to her. He went past the park entrance and turned back around. This time, he was facing the same direction as her with no one behind him. He rolled down the window and slowed.

"Hey! Mary Margaret! Hop in. I'll give you a ride home."

"No thanks. I'm almost there."

"Mary Margaret. Please get in. I want to talk to you."

"That's OK. I'm good."

He looked up and saw somebody coming up behind him. "Mary Margaret," he pleaded. "Please get in before I get in an accident."

"Oh, alright. Pull over." He did and she got in his car. "What's the emergency?"

"Not yet. I have a stop to make."

"I didn't get in to run errands with you. Let me out."

John pulled into a shopping plaza and parked in front of a liquor store. "Please don't get out. I'll be right back." She sat there and waited for him. He came back with a bottle in a brown paper bag and got back in the car. "Oh. You're still here." John said to her. "Why didn't you get out? I figured I'd have to chase you all over town."

"You said please."

He sighed a big, exasperated sigh. "How come you're not staying to watch the fireworks?"

"I don't need to. I can see them from my house."

"Would you allow me to stay and watch them from your house?"

"Sure. I'm not sure how much fun you'll have by yourself."

"Please don't bust my balls over this. It's been a long day. Please watch them with me. I have wine." He said and gave her the brown paper bag. She pulled out the bottle, looked at the label and nodded. Shortly John pulled in her driveway. They got out and she pushed the code, and the door went up.

"You can see them best from the front. There's a couple of lounge chairs under that tarp over there. They shouldn't be too dirty. You can put them in the grass or on the driveway. I'll go inside and grab a corkscrew and a couple of glasses. Stella came out when Mary Margaret returned, and he had the chairs placed on the lawn. He bowed and made a sweeping gesture with his arm. John took the corkscrew and glasses from her.

"Have a seat. They weren't dirty at all. I'll take it from here. You just have to relax. That's all that's required from you for the rest of the evening. Relax."

He opened the bottle and poured them each a glass. He handed her both so he could sit. She passed his back. He said, "a toast. To peace and quiet with no crowds, until dark anyway."

"I'll drink to that," Mary Margaret said, and clinked glasses. They sat in silence for a while, enjoying the wine. She finally spoke.

"So, John, what's up? What's so important?"

"I forget. I had a whole laundry list of things I wanted to bring up, but it's too nice a night to spend it out-thinking you. Let's just enjoy the wine."

"Out-thinking me?"

"I say one thing, you think another. If I don't watch myself, we end up having two different conversations."

"Yeah. Let's avoid that."

It was approaching dusk as they sat and enjoyed the wine. It was too early for the fireworks; the first glass loosened their tongues and mellowed their attitudes.

"Why were you so mean to me today? I wanted to buy something, and you wouldn't let me."

"I'll be honest. Whether or not I'm interested in you, you always acted interested in me. Then I see you with your girlfriend and it makes me think you're a liar. All this interest in me is insincere. You have a girlfriend. I was strictly being petty. You can have fifty girlfriends. That's none of my business.

"You travel a lot; I bet there's a girlfriend in every city. Anyway, I see you with Evelynne, talking about what would look good over her couch. That made me mad, and I have no right to be. You're free to have 100 girlfriends. I got mad at myself for getting angry.

"The fact she said my work looked like someone vomited on the canvas didn't help. I shouldn't have gotten mad about that, either. It's abstract art and each person is supposed to make their own interpretation of it anyway." Night was falling and the insects came out. She swatted the mosquito on her forearm. A smear of blood remained.

"I thought you brought her by to show me, I don't know, that I was a minnow among many minnows. There's a lot of women more pleasant than I am, I know that. I don't blame you for wanting to be with a woman, you're supposed to. You're a guy. I really don't know what rankled me. Maybe it was Evelynne." *Maybe it's because I'm jealous and I don't want to be.*

"It was just like 'Evelynne, darling, how about this one? Won't it look nice over the couch?' I wanted to barf. Next time I'll grab a canvas and puke all over it for real. Maybe that's why we're called starving artists; we fight with all our customers and go home broke. I should say I'm sorry. No should about it, I'm sorry I was so mean to you. You didn't deserve it."

"Would you allow me to explain today?"

"Why are you asking my permission for everything?"

"I need to figure out if you want to hear what I have to say, otherwise you stop listening and it's just blah, blah, blah."

"God, what happened to me? I used to be a nice person. I used to be a good person. Now I'm just a bitch." Mary Margaret lamented. "Maybe you're stirring up feelings in me I don't want to feel."

"You still are. Buried under that cantankerous exterior is soft and mushy inside." *She admitted to feeling something for me. Well, what do you know.* "I'm sure of it. I feel the need to explain my involvement with Evelynne. It's not exactly what it looked like. I know her from work. She's one of the Operation Managers, and when I first got here, she offered to show me around. I took her up on it, and we dated a bit, but I'm here to do a job, not socialize. I told her so, and she wasn't happy about it.

"The other day I was under a desk trying to organize cables and connections and she came in. She was talking and I just kept saying 'yeah, uh-huh,' and she brought up going to Founder's Day. I guess I said 'yeah, uh-huh' one too many times because she asked me to go with her and I said yes.

"We go, and she's all over me, holding my hand, trying to hug me. I tried to avoid your booth, but I got mixed up and ended up in front of it. I didn't know you were there. As soon as I saw you, she started to get all touchy-feely, laying it on thick. Saying something about her couch probably made you think I spent a lot of time on it. I only said that because she kept going on and on about that hideous rope thing, and saying something about your painting was just to goof on her. I knew she'd hate it. I thought I'd buy it and you refused to sell it to me. You refused to sell me anything."

"If you want something I'll just give it to you."

"I didn't know you had a history with her, or I wouldn't have stopped."

"History? What history?"

"She said you were weird, and I should avoid you at all costs."

"She was a queen bee in high school, and I wasn't part of the hive. How did you get away from her?"

"Pass me that bottle. I need another drink to get through that story. All I can say is I'm going to hell for sure. I should have gotten two bottles of wine. This one's done."

"There's another inside. It's on the counter."

"You're empty. I'll go grab it," he said, and went inside. He came back and asked for the corkscrew. He filled her glass and sat back in his chaise, crossed his legs at the ankle and contentedly sipped his glass. "This is nice, real nice. Way better than Founder's Day. We don't even need fireworks."

"So, what happened to Evelynne?"

"I lied my face off. I told her I was a Vietnam war vet, and fireworks would trigger my PTSD so I had to go home and sit in the dark. I left her with some of her friends."

101

"You are going to hell." Mary Margaret laughed. They sat as the night closed in, the fireworks almost due to go off.

"Would you allow me one more question?"

"Yes. Then you have to be quiet."

"What's your last name?

"That's what you want to know?"

"You once told me it was Welch. I snagged one of your business cards today and it says Miller."

"My business cards were on the table? Damn that Jason. Were they titled Godzilla Studios? Miller was my last name before I got married. After I got married it was Welch. When we divorced Casey was small, and I wanted to have the same last name as hers while she was in school. Ben didn't care, neither did Sheila. Once I started selling my artwork, I was still using Welch. I thought about changing it back, I even had business cards printed up, but after my mom died I didn't. I didn't go back to Miller because it made me sad. I'd be the only Miller left."

"Just one more question. Last one. Please. I promise."

"Last one. I mean it."

"Can I hold your hand?"

"What? Why?"

"No more questions, remember? I'll tell you after the fireworks."

They stopped talking and waited for the fireworks. He held her hand. John didn't do anything with it. He didn't try to stroke the tender vee that her index finger and thumb made, he didn't squeeze it, he just held it. The night was creeping in, announced by the sound of the leaf peepers, crickets and other things that came alive in the dark. The fireworks started. The breeze carried the noise and colorful sparks until the display was practically over their heads. They had to lean the lounge chairs all the way back. The booms were so loud it made their spines vibrate. When it was all over, they stayed reclined and looked at the now black sky for stars.

"Are your ears still ringing? That's the closest I've ever been to fireworks. It might have been too close. I thought the sparks were going to fall out of the sky and set your hair on fire." John said, still holding her hand. *I love this hand,* the thought ran through his head.

"Usually, they blow the other the other way, but that was really cool. It was like our own personal show, and no traffic to deal with afterwards. You're still holding my hand. Why?"

"I don't know exactly how to explain why, but I'll try. Sometimes, when you hold hands with a girl you marvel at the smoothness, the softness, how delicate it feels. Well, yours don't. They feel like hands that work. Not like you have big calluses or anything, but they're not shy hands. They're strong hands. Like if you're trapped in a burning building with someone, I'd rather it be you than some simpering flower. You have hands that do things. Your hand tells a story. It tells me you're strong, and brave. I admire that."

"Huh. They say all that?"

"Yes. That's why I like to hang around you. Life is always in motion and your life moves to places I've never been before. Like the Emergency Room. I've never taken a woman to the Emergency Room before."

"That wasn't a date, John."

"Oh, I know, but it was still fun. You had to go to the ER because you were busy living your life and something happened. Your dog shows up out of the blue. Things like that."

"I tripped over a paint can and hit my head. I wasn't juggling while riding a unicycle and fell."

"I know, but still. I don't even know what you were doing in your garage. You live life without worrying about breaking a nail."

"That's true. That's probably why my hands look like I've been digging potatoes. Anytime Casey gives me a gift it always includes a manicure, and she has to take me, otherwise I won't go."

He laughed. "Digging potatoes. I've never heard that before."

"I have to go inside and pee. The mosquitoes are eating me alive." Mary Margaret said.

"I'll clean up out here and meet you inside. I need to use the restroom as well, if you don't mind."

"I don't mind. You drank a lot of wine, I bet you really have to go."

"I had help. Go."

She went inside, did her business and came out into the kitchen. She found John rinsing out the wine glasses. "It's free. First door on the left."

"No need. I watered the bushes." He followed her into the family room. He stopped and studied a painting. It was a landscape. This is you? MMMiller? It's beautiful, very 'Hudson River School.'"

She approached and stood next to him and looked at the painting. "Thanks for the compliment. I was going for that 'airy' feel so prevalent in those paintings. I also liked the Pre Raphaelites; I spent a lot of time making my friends wear costumes I put together from thrift stores, like old wedding dresses and stuff. I took things from the Drama Club. Maybe that is is why I always fall back on using three names, like Fredric George Stephens or John Williams Waterhouse. Then I went to Art School, and they blasted everything I knew about art out of the water."

"That picture I painted in high school. It won a Gold Key at the state competition."

"In high school? I don't believe it. This is beautiful."

"They were good enough to get me a scholarship here to the local University in the School of Fine Arts. That was good enough to get me a job in the Art Department doing inventory. You have no idea of the sheer amount of things

104

they have in their collections. I've been counting stuff for years. For every two months of doing inventory on how many gallons of paint or pounds of clay we had, I'd see the Rembrandt drawings they have in the archive. I worked there for years, all while Casey was in school."

"Why did you stop?"

"My father died when I was sixteen, my mom when Casey was sixteen, about ten years ago. I was glad she had the time to know her grandmother, my mom. Anyway, my parents were in the insurance business. They believed in it. There was a lot of it. My mother never spent one penny of the huge chunk of change she inherited when my dad died.

"She already had a job, doing the things my dad did. So that was invested, and when she died, between her policies and all those years that money from my dad was invested I was no longer required to work, and Casey's education was taken care of. I decided had breathed my last breath of dusty air and quit." Mary Margaret went over and sat on the couch. John joined her.

"Where was I? I was able to get health insurance through Ben. I pay for it, but I'm part of a group. He was working at my parent's agency and took it over when she died. I planned on getting back into serious painting, but I couldn't seem to catch a wave of inspiration. I was wandering around the grocery store, and I see Caitlin, the realtor. She asked me if I could throw some sort of predominately blue large abstract together in two weeks. I said sure, and looked on You Tube and found a technique.

"I did it in my garage; that's how Jason got involved. It was too big a canvas for one person. After he finished the lawn, he came in to see what I wanted. I took a broom and swept Jason down I brushed him good. I didn't want grass clippings in the painting. We mixed and poured and tilted an abstract painting in tones of blue. I had it on a couple of sawhorses in the garage. I got one of those pop-up tent things, and cheap shower curtains from the dollar store and stapled them to the canopy. It made pretty good drying tent. It kept the dust off and dried clean. That was the start of MMWELCH, FINE ARTIST AND CRAFTSMAN."

"You have no family here? No aunts or uncles? No cousins?"

"No. Just Casey, and Ben and his family. This wine is making me sleepy," she yawned. "How about you?"

"I'm so tired I'm too tired to do anything about it."

"Yeah. The fireworks were pretty good. I'm glad I was able to stay awake for them. Evelynne is so far away right now. Want to squeeze up here? I can take the cushions off." She threw them on the floor. "Come up and take a rest." He had just enough room if they both laid sideways. He laid down in front her, but she was already asleep. He kicked off his shoes and told himself he was just going to grab a few zzzs and be gone before she woke up.

John woke few hours later. He had a headache from the wine and his muscles ached from the cramped position he slept in. John remembered from when she cut her head where she kept her Tylenol.

He found a few bottles of different types of pain reliever, selected one, and took some with a glass of water. Her brought some over to her to leave for when she woke up.

"What are you doing?" She said, half awake.

"Leaving. Here, take these. You'll thank me in the morning." He put them in her hand with a glass of water. She swallowed them; he left the water and two capsules on the coffee table for the morning. "It's time for me to go." Mary Margaret grabbed his collar, brought his head down and kissed him on the lips. She mumbled something and fell back asleep.

What was that? Did she just kiss me? Why does she say one thing but act the opposite? John thought. He felt a chill run through him, and he liked it.

John let himself out and went home to a real bed. He must be getting old; he valued a good night's sleep more than waking up next to a pretty girl. God, he was old. John wouldn't know if she was a real bitch before her first cup of coffee. In his head Mary Margaret was charming and perfect. He wasn't willing to surrender his delusion yet.

Mary Margaret woke later to the sunshine coming through the blinds, it was sliced up and covered her in little strips. It was hot. She took the last two tablets and gratefully drank the water. She got up and peed, vaguely remembered John leaving. Mary Margaret didn't understand him leaving, or she felt about it. Part of her was glad, she had a bit of a hangover and didn't feel like being pleasant; part of her was insulted. He had the perfect excuse to stay. She remembered how nice an evening they spent watching the fireworks and he didn't try to make it more than it was. Did she want more? Such a thought required more brain power than she had at the time and set the thought aside.

***

He got the message about Mary Margaret not wanting more loud and clear. Maybe it was her ego, or the teen age girl that still resided inside her heart, but he should have found it hard to leave. John should have woken her up and made a declaration about not wanting to leave, but would because that's what she wanted. Instead, he snuck out like some no-name one night stand, getting in bed with Cindy Crawford only to wake up next to Cindy Brady. It didn't matter, nothing happened.

That should make her happy, but she didn't feel happy. *All this thinking is causing my headache to worsen and making me nauseous,* she thought. *I gotta go back to bed before I puke. Is there a canvas nearby I could vomit on and give to Evelynne?* Mary Margaret let Stella out, and when she came back in, she jumped on the couch waiting for her owner to lie down. Rather than make the effort of getting to her room and her real bed, she laid on the couch. Stella curled up and they both fell asleep.

Mary Margaret woke for good around eleven; she slept away her headache and she was hungry. She got up and straightened up the cushions and let Stella out again, leaving the screen open enough for Stella to come back inside when she was ready. Mary Margaret made coffee and looked in the fridge. It was as bare as old mother Hubbard's cupboard. There wasn't even bread for toast. She frowned and shut the door. She heard the garage door open. Casey appeared at the window of the kitchen door, knocking for her to let her in. Mary Margaret opened the door and sat back at the kitchen table.

107

"Hey, Mom, I brought you a bagel." Casey said as she sat across from her mother. She slid the bag containing the bagel to her mother. She looked inside and looked at Casey.

"Bless you, Casey. There's nothing to eat in this house, and I'm starving."

"Happy to do it, Mom. Are you OK? You look a little green around the gills, and you slept in your clothes. By the way, don't wear that in public anymore. It's not a good look. It's downright embarrassing."

Mary Margaret finished chewing her bagel before she answered. She held the bagel up and said, "starve a cold, feed a hangover."

Casey looked around the kitchen and noticed two empty wine bottles. "Mom. You didn't. You didn't come home and drink two bottles of wine by yourself, did you?"

"Of course not. I'd have my head in the toilet if I drank that much. I had help. John picked me up when I was walking home. He was talking about the fireworks, and why I didn't stay to watch them. I said I could see them from my house. He stopped and got some wine and we watched from the front yard. The wind blew them right over our heads. It was pretty cool."

"John was here? How late did he stay?"

"I'm not sure. We fell asleep. He left before I woke up."

"Oh. I didn't come over to talk about your love life, anyway. I came over to talk about mine."

"You have a love life? Yeah, let's talk about that, it has to be way more exciting than mine."

"It is. I think I'm in love, for real this time." Casey said, blushing bright red as she said the words out loud.

"That guy I met yesterday? Doctor Greene? It happened kind of quick, don't you think?

"Not really. I know him from work. Yesterday was the first time we went out as a couple, but we've been involved for a while. He finds out when I take my breaks and manages to always up be in the same place at the same time."

"Lunch, coffee, dinner, it's like we were dating but only at work. Both of our schedules didn't make going out on a regular date easy, but I think we didn't take it outside if there wasn't a point to it. There's a point to it now. That's why you met him. It's getting sort of serious. He asked me if I wanted to be his girlfriend, and if I did, that meant we didn't see other people. He's willing to make the commitment if I was, so I said yes. I have a boyfriend, his name is Seth Greene. Seth Greene has a girlfriend named Casey Welch. We are officially a couple."

Mary Margaret stood up and hugged Casey. "Wow. Congratulations. So, he's the one?"

"Yeah, I think he is the one."

"He seemed very nice; he has a kind of confidence that makes everyone around him at ease," Mary Margaret said. "I like him."

"Wow. I can't believe it. No grilling, no prying, no third degree?"

"No. You'll tell me about him when you're ready. Tell me what you want me to know."

"He's from Milwaukee. He's one of four kids, second oldest. He's an anesthesiologist doing a pediatric fellowship. His dad is a doctor, his mother a nurse. He's just the nicest guy. He must have gone to etiquette class; he holds open doors for me, if I call an Uber, he meets the driver and takes a picture of him for safety's sake."

"Or he's watched too many episodes of Dateline."

"He comes from white bread, corn fed, all American, normal people."

"I didn't scare him, did I?"

"He found your eccentricity charming. He liked you; he thinks you're an old hippy and I didn't contradict him. I found you an embarrassment. Please don't leave the house in those clothes again, Mom."

"Got it. Studio only."

"Not even there. Throw them out. Don't bother washing them. I'm not kidding."

"Yes, Casey. I understand."

"I love you, Mom. I feel good about this." She got up and hugged Mary Margaret.

"I love you too, Casey, and I'm so happy for you. He seems like a good guy." Mary Margaret said and smiled at her daughter. Her adult, grown up, in love daughter.

"He is, Mom, he is. It was nice having coffee with you. I've got to run." On her way out the door she let John in.

"Hello, Mary Margaret. Aren't you a vision first thing in the morning?"

"That's a poor excuse for sarcasm."

"Have you looked in the mirror?"

She let that pass because it hurt her head to come up with a clever response. "What brings you by?"

"I brought donuts. I wasn't sure what shape you'd be after we drank ourselves blotto. A sugar rush sometimes helps. I'm going to make some coffee. Would you another cup?"

"Yeah, why not? If it wasn't for caffeine and carbs, I don't know if I'd be awake right now. Let's throw some sugar into the mix. You look pretty good considering the amount of wine you drank."

"Practice, Mary Margaret, Practice. And a shower."

"I agree about the shower, but first coffee and a donut."

He served them their coffee and sat down. John took a chocolate glazed donut, split in half, and handed her a piece. "Casey looks good." He said.

"Oh, Oh, Oh!" Mary Margaret said. "Casey came over and made an announcement. She has a boyfriend."

"She does? When did she find time for one of those?"

"She met him at work. A doctor. Their romance has been hospital based, that's where they spend the most time. He asked her to be his girlfriend. If she said yes that meant they didn't see other people. They were at the Founder's Day fireworks as an official couple."

"That's exciting news. I'm glad for her. I'm glad she didn't model her social life after mother. She seemed like her priority was getting through school. Her narrow scope and focus reminded me of you. I'm glad she wasn't taking notes and left herself some room for fun."

"How do I respond to that? Do I get mad or agree with you?"

"Agree. It's too nice a day to be angry. Want to go for a drive? I've never been anyplace outside a half hour of here. Where could we go?"

"What are you in the mood for? Water or mountains? Hiking or sightseeing? Wine tour? Boat ride? That's the only benefit of this podunk town. Two hours in any direction is a complete change of scenery."

"The water, and just for sightseeing. Nothing stressful. But first you need some water for a shower, and if it's no trouble, a change of clothes."

"The shower, I'm aware of. The clothes, Casey made me promise to burn. Give me a half hour. Have another cup of coffee, and I'll be right out."

Hah! He thought. *A woman who can get ready in a half hour. I'll believe when I see it.*

Mary Margaret was back with five minutes to spare. Granted, she didn't blow dry her hair, she just fluffed it out and twisted it up on her head. She wore a fitted black tee and a pair of black shorts. John admired her strong arms and her smooth legs. When she tried, she could be a real knockout. He was almost glad that she chose to dress like her wardrobe came from Goodwill. In fact, most of it did, but in an age where women compensated for aging with sharp dressing and top-notch accessories, he found her minimalist approach refreshing.

They took his car, and both put on their sunglasses. John laughed and said she looked like a movie star. She laughed and said "who? Old Yeller?" It made him mad she always threw herself under the bus for a laugh. He wasn't sure if it was all in good fun, or she was taking the shot before any body else could. Mary Margaret was old enough to have been around the block a few times, and he didn't doubt she had her share of heartache and trauma. Trauma? He meant drama.

In about an hour and a half they came to a toll bridge. From the toll booth all he could see was the bridge. A suspension bridge, it looked like the bridge rose impossibly straight up into the air. He could not see the other side of the bridge or the land where it connected.

He looked at Mary Margaret doubtfully. "Where are you taking me?"

"Canada. Almost."

He had no choice but to go forward. As he started the ascent he had a chance to see why there was a need for a bridge. Below was a large expanse of water dotted with outcroppings of land, some large enough for mansions, some for camps, some covered in trees where no buildings were spotted, the only evidence of human existence was a dock or a yellow kayak. He had to keep his eyes on the road. A tractor trailer was tight on his ass and he couldn't appreciate the geography below. He started the decent and saw the land on the other side.

"Take your first right after the bridge, and a left at the T."

He took the first right after the bridge, but instead of taking a left he pulled into the parking lot of a hardware store. A colorful display of plastic Adirondack chairs lined the entrance.

"Explain what we're doing, please." John asked.

"I know you know where we are, I saw you reading the signs."

"We're in Canada?"

"No. You must have missed the 'Last Exit Before Canada' one. That bridge crosses the St. Lawrence River, and where we are is called the Thousand Islands. This is Wesley Island. I figured I'd show you the rich side, and then the average Joe side. That has a lot of shops and touristy stuff. Take that left. I'll show you what I mean."

He drove on until she told him to pull over.

"Right here is part of the golf course. There's a country club on this side, too. There's a lunch type place, and a fining dining restaurant. There's a nice view of the castle, too."

"Castle?"

"Drive on, Mr. Adams." She directed. They drove on and came to a 'cart crossing' sign. "More golf course." The drove past the two restaurants and came to a fork. Either choice took them past earth toned condominiums.

"Go to the left for now. These are owned by people, some who only come up once a year, and others live here all summer. A lot of these people are assholes. They ride around on their bikes, or roller blades and in their golf carts and take down your license plate if you go too fast, so watch the speed bumps. It goes around in a big loop, but the upper part isn't on the water; those condos come with a boat slip."

"How do you know all about this place?"

"Casey. All through elementary school her best friend was Andrea Molinaro. Her mom and three kids stayed all summer, Mr. Molinaro stayed in town and worked. He came up on Friday and spent the weekends here. They own an island, too, but have to share it with her brother and sister. They bought the condo because he couldn't take spending his free time with the horde of kids that ran wild. Casey spent a lot of time up here, and sometimes I drove up to get her or drop her off.

"Really lovely people, they invited me up here to spend a week plenty of times. I only spent the night once. They had a wedding at the club, so I came up and watched the kids. Sunday we went out on their boat, they gave me the tour.

113

Lots of history up here. The Molinaro's moved out of state. We lost touch. I don't know if they still come up here." He followed the road until the came back to the entrance.

"Now, go to the right of the stone wall. Take that gravel road until the end. We'll get out and walk to the dock. That's the best view of the castle." He did as he was told. They got out and started down the path. "Now, if anybody asks what we're doing, we are checking out the real estate. We might be interested in buying a property."

A five-minute walk brought them to the docks. They walked out to the end. She pointed across the water. "See? The castle? It's called Boldt Castle."

"You're right. It is a castle. A real castle." John nodded, surprised.

"What? You thought I was kidding?" Mary Margaret asked.

"I was thinking more along the lines somebody built a castle, a gross, ostentatious, nouveau riche structure to impress the boaters and tourists. A 'look at me, I own a castle and you don't kind of castle.'"

"No. It truly is a real castle. There's a whole story behind it. You ready to cross the bridge again? I'll drive, you can look. We can check out the other side. Maybe sit down and have a sandwich. I'll give you a brief synopsis of the area."

"Sounds good," John said and followed her back to the car. There was an older gentleman waiting for them. He had very small dog on the end of a leash.

"Excuse me, but you're trespassing on private property." He said in a firm voice, like they were a couple of bums from the wrong side of the bridge.

"No. Excuse *me*." Mary Margaret said. She had a tone in her voice John had never heard. She sounded like a rich person who wasn't used to being questioned. "We are looking at properties, and the realtor thought we might want to look at these slips to see if they would be big enough for our boat."

The man's face showed he was weakening in his position but was committed to it and going to follow through. "You should check out what's available on the lower loop. You can park your boat right in front of your house."

"Yes, that's true, but considering the number of kids and traffic, that's not the place to go if you're looking to get away from it all, is it?"

"Whose place are you looking at over here?" The man asked.

"That's a question for the realtor."

"Who's your realtor?"

"Bonnie Ellis."

John watch their discussion like he was watching a tennis match.

"Tell me," Mary Margaret asked. "I see you have a dog. Does the Homeowner's Association have any stipulation as to the size or breed of dog?"

"Not that I know of," he admitted.

"Oh, good. I was afraid there would discrimination because we have two pit bulls, Tank and Chaos, they're our babies. Your little dog would be a snack to our boys. It was very nice talking to you. We'll move the car, so we won't be trespassing any longer. Goodbye," she said and stepped around the man.

"Here, John. My turn to drive." She got in the driver's seat, rolled the window down, and spoke to the man. "Thank you for your time. I hope to be neighbors real soon!"

She turned the car around and drove off. Once they were out of view she pulled over and started laughing. He started laughing until tears gathered in his eyes.

"Oh, Mary Margaret, you kill me. How do you make up shit like that? 'We need to see if the slip is big enough for our boat. Our two pit bulls, Tank and Chaos.' He folded like a cheap suit. How'd you know the realtor's name?"

"Every place on the market has the sign out with the name Bonnie Ellis. I just notice things, I retain things for future use. This time it came in handy. I have a whole brain full of useless crap."

"You even changed your voice. You sounded like you were a Rockefeller. Or a Kennedy."

"Well, he was an asshole. That's why I dress like I do. I don't want people asking me questions. If I had on what I had on yesterday he would have called the cops. Today I look 'presentable.' That guy felt he could talk to me like that. If I looked like I did yesterday, he'd be too scared to approach me. I like it better that way. Now, we're going to go over the bridge. I hope you're not afraid of heights."

The return trip over the bridge allowed John to see the river, the islands popping up everywhere, each different from the others. He saw boats of all different sizes leave their wakes behind them. The sun bounced back from the surface of the river so bright it was almost impossible to see anything without sunglasses. They exited the bridge, she made a left, and headed into the small town of Center Bay. It was a popular place for those without the money to live on the other side. She found a parking spot right on Main Street. It was late Sunday afternoon and the weekenders were clearing out, leaving the street without the usual crowds.

"Since it's Sunday, a lot of the stores close by seven. If you want to buy anything, we need to get busy. Otherwise let's window shop. The restaurants are open, I think until nine. It all may have changed, I don't know. It'd be good if we could grab something to eat outside and look at the river."

They walked down Main Street and window shopped but didn't go in any stores. They neared a gift shop with the door propped open. Mary Margaret went inside, and John followed her. "Look around," she told him. "I'll talk to the cashier about our dinner options."

John wandered around the store filled with typical gift shop things. He stopped in front of a wall of clothes. Everything from tees and sweatshirts to baby and pet clothes. Every item had a complementary version in tie-dye. He found a dog leash advertising the Thousand Islands; it didn't look too garish or cheap. He went to the register to pay, behind Mary Margaret. She moved aside and he stepped up. She looked at the leash and laughed. "Stella will love that."

"It's for you," John said. She laughed again.

"Thank you. Nadia here," she said, referring to the clerk, "said across the street is a place on the water, 'Rumrunner's,' or a steak place at the end of the street. Fancy, but no view. I vote for casual and a view."

116

"Same," he said as she bagged his leash, and they went back outside.

She put her bag on the floor behind the driver's seat and got in. Mary Margaret drove a short distance, took a left and saw the water. She parked, grabbed the bag and pointed up, and they ascended the stairs.

"Hey. What did you buy?"

"You'll see." She spoke to the hostess, and they were seated at a table on the deck; the water brilliant below them. "Here," she said, and passed the bag over to him. He opened it up and pulled out a souvenir coffee mug.

He laughed. "Thank you. Now I'll think about how beautiful today was every time I use it."

"That's the point. Before Casey went to nursing school, we travel a bit. I chaperoned the French Club's trip to Paris. I was a terrible chaperone. I spent all my free time at the Louvre. Anyway, instead of buying tee shirts, we'd buy a coffee mug. That way we'd start the day with a happy memory. We used to have quite a collection, but I haven't been anywhere in so long, it's dwindled quite a bit. The other one is mine."

"Thank you, Mary Margaret. I don't think I've ever been the gift of such spontaneous generosity."

"What does that mean?"

"It means thank you. I'm surprised you gave me a gift. You didn't have to, you just did it."

"It's just a mug, John, not a Rolex."

"Maybe the grand gesture is overrated. This is more than enough." He said and smiled a genuine smile. She didn't think he looked 'old,' when he smiled, he looked quite youthful. Yes, when his smile reached his eyes it settled into familiar grooves, but kind ones, ones caused by laughter. His brown eyes were clear, and he still had all his teeth, she noted.

It was later in the day, and she could see the start of a five o'clock shadow. This was really the first time she studied his face, her mind assessing it from an artist's viewpoint. She thought of her friends who dressed up and posed for her all those years ago and smiled. Mary Margaret thought she'd like to wrap him in a sheet and give him a big book, like a dictionary, and have his other hand up in the air, she was philosophizing to the masses.

"What are you smiling about?" John asked. He noticed her looking at him.

"The truth? I was thinking about wrapping you in a sheet and painting you as Aristotle."

"I like the wrapping me in a sheet part, we'd have to rehearse that." He laughed.

The waitress broke the moment and delivered their food; she had a BLT and lemonade, he a grilled chicken sandwich with iced tea. They ate in silence, watching the boats go by. "Look." She said and pointed at the channel. A freighter passed by.

"Wow." John said. "It's not just a resort town. You have a castle and shipping lanes. Why do you have castle again?"

"It's a long story, but around 1900 some rich guy, his name was George Boldt, came up from the City bought the island as a wedding gift to his wife. He even had it carved in the shape of a heart, that's why it's called Heart Island. There's a power building, and the smaller castle for the kids was completed first. The boathouse is huge. From what I know, it had only the best. Italian marble, hand carved woodwork, all of it. He brought workers from Europe. The plan was to live in the smaller castle while they finished the big one.

"It was almost finished and one winter his wife died, and he walked away from it all. He never came back. Over time, people tore out all the good stuff and looted the place. It fell into a huge pile of disrepair. There was a lot of trouble over who actually owned it. The Seaway Authority? Center Bay? Canada? The State? There was some talk about turning it into a casino. In the end, I'm not sure who owns it now, but over the past thirty years they have been restoring it as a tourist attraction. I think it's pretty nice now, they have tours and a ferry that takes people back in forth runs all summer. It has been rehabbed to its former glory, from what I understand, or that's what they're working towards. It's popular for weddings. There's another castle, Singer Castle, from the sewing machine

118

people. It's further out somewhere and just a pile of stone. I went by the island once ages ago, and it looked spooky then. I can't imagine what it looks now."

"That's amazing. Two castles. What else?"

"You know how this place is called 'Rumrunners'? It's because of Prohibition. Alcohol was smuggled in from Canada. All these little islands hold lots of secrets, I imagine."

"I had no idea all this was less than two hours away. This was a great idea for an afternoon trip."

"I'm glad you enjoyed it."

"And now, whenever I have coffee, I'll recall how much fun I had."

"Exactly."

They were quiet for a moment, each taking in the surroundings. Some bigger islands were located in the Bay. Some families shared an island with other families, some families had their own sprawling estates. Boats, yachts, jet ski's, canoes, and kayaks tied up to the docks. Mary Margaret was amazed at the sheer amount of money here. Old money, many islands have been in families for generations. If there was that kind of money in this puny little bay, imagine San Diego. Or Miami. Mind boggling was her assessment.

"What's on your mind?" John asked her. He learned that even if Mary Margaret wasn't speaking, it didn't mean she wasn't thinking.

"Just about the haves. The problems of the have-nots seem so far away. I doubt people up here even think about them."

"I was just sitting here enjoying the sun on my face, and you're thinking about social inequity."

"I was enjoying the sun, too."

"Mary Margaret. Be my girlfriend."

"Nope. You're ruining a perfectly good friendship. Quit pushing it."

"Why not? I like you and you like me. It's that simple. You're the one that making it complicated."

He watched her physical appearance change right in front of him. Her face drained of all color. She pushed back in her chair; her eyes wildly searched for the exit. It was only by looking at her eyes could he see the truth. They were opened wide, bright with unshed tears. Mary Margaret looked like she was backed into a corner, like she was trapped in a burning building. She was scared.

"Hey," he said quietly, and reached for her hand. "Mary Margaret. Look at me. Mary Margaret. Please. Look at me. It's OK."

She looked at him, blinking a few times to clear her head. "Oh. John," was all she said.

He waved to the hostess, signaling for the check. He got it, looked at it and took money from his pocket and left it on the table. He got up and reached for her; she remained seated as if unaware he moved. He took her arm and helped her up. He thanked the hostess and ushered Mary Margaret out to the car. "Come here, Mary Margaret. Let me hold you." She did as he asked, only she grabbed him and held him tight. "I don't know what you're afraid of, but it's okay. You're here with me. I'll keep you safe. I promise."

"Oh, John, I'm sorry. We were having such a great day and I ruin it by having a panic attack."

John took her face in his hands. "Look at me." She lifted her watery eyes up to his. "I'm not the enemy. I'm your friend. Yes, I'd like more, but I don't need it. It doesn't make me care any less about you." He held her face and kissed her, and to his surprise she kissed him back. Granted, they were small kisses and held no promises, but her lips were soft and smooth. He backed off but to his surprise she reached up and kissed him again. When she was finished, she released him and smiled. When he was sure she was done kissing him he asked for the keys. Mary Margaret gave them to him, and he got her in the car. He seated himself and started the car. Before he pulled out, he spoke to her.

"Hey, look at me." He reached over and jiggled her leg. Mary Margaret turned to face him. She looked embarrassed. She was still fighting back tears.

"Whatever it is, it's alright. I won't press and ask any questions. Just give me your hand."

"OK," she said in small voice. He pulled out and took her hand. He was glad they already went over the bridge. They drove home in silence; he periodically squeezed her hand. He wanted her to know whatever it was, it was okay. She was okay.

When he pulled in her driveway it was getting dark. She finally spoke.

"Do you know some ancient cultures thought dusk was the time of day that the veil that separated the living and the dead was at its thinnest, so people were scared to be out in it?"

"No, I did not. Let's hurry and get inside, I bet Stella really has to go."

Stella met them at the door. She barked once and ran by them onto the grass and went potty. She came back and gave them a proper greeting. Stella followed them inside looking for some ear scratching and belly rubs. Mary Margaret went in and sat on the couch. Stella jumped up, not used to being ignored. She got some perfunctory attention but not enough to satisfy her. She whined and pushed her nose under her owner's hand. John looked at Mary Margaret. All he could think of was how sad she looked. He wanted to help her, but he didn't know how.

"I think I'll take her for a walk before I leave. It's going to get dark soon and you shouldn't be out alone, walking around after dark. I'll see how she likes her new leash." He clipped her leash and took her out.

***

"Stella, tell me." John asked. "You've known her longer than I have. Do you know what's wrong? What is it that sends her from smiling one minute to terror the next?"

Stella stopped and looked at John. He thought Stella wanted to tell him something, instead she squatted and pooped. She scratched the grass when she finished. John leaned over and picked it up.

"That it, Stella? Are you trying to tell me I'm full of shit?" He said to her as they walked on. John went around the block trying to figure out what he should do. Leave? Leave her alone? Talk to her? Try to get her to open up, or just put her to bed and sleep on the couch, chasing away any monsters that happened in the night? He still hadn't reached an answer when he reached her door. He followed Stella in and figured he'd just have to wing it.

"We're back," he called out. Mary Margaret was sitting in the same spot she was in when he left. He sat next to her. "Hey, Mary Margaret. I'm going to get going. I thought today was a great day. Whatever I did, I'm sorry." He watched her look down and avoid his eyes. Her shoulders sagged, and she looked utterly defeated. He automatically reached out and pulled her into his arms. She felt boneless. He held her tighter and she started to cry. Instead of pushing him away she clung to him with all her strength. He held her until she was all cried out.

"I'm going to grab some tissues. Be right back." John said and went into the bathroom.

Mary Margaret looked at him when he returned. Her eyes were puffy and red, but whatever dark place she went, she was back. She took the tissues and wiped her face. Mary Margaret blew her nose and gave an embarrassed laugh. "Well, that's attractive," she said of the wad of snotty tissues in front of her.

"Look. I don't know what happened and I don't want to. I was going to go but I wish you'd let me stay for a bit, if only for my own peace of mind. You really scared me."

"I must have had a panic attack," she said.

"OK, sure." *That was no panic attack,* he thought. *I don't know what rabbit hole you went down, but it scared the shit out of me.* "Well, please let me stay for a few more minutes. I've got a big week ahead of me, and I won't be able to get anything done if I'm worrying about you."

"That's alright. I think it passed, but if you want to stay and watch tv for a bit, you can," she said and handed him the remote. He found something to watch and leaned back next to her, on the alert for any tension emanating from her, but he detected none and relaxed a bit himself. He noticed Stella looking at him.

122

"What's up with Stella?"

"You're on her side."

He got up and sat on the other side. She only wanted him switch seats; she didn't ask him to leave.

John stayed for an hour, trying casually to look at her without her catching him. Mary Margaret seemed OK, tired if anything. He wasn't lying when he said a big day tomorrow, but he was loathe to leave her if she wasn't telling him the truth when she said she was okay. The program ended, and he got up.

"I do have to go, I've got an early meeting, but you'll be okay after I go, right?'

"I'll be fine. I'm sorry I ruined our afternoon. It was a lot of fun until I lost it." Mary Margaret apologized.

"It was a great afternoon; it was a lot of fun regardless of a little glitch. The most fun I've had since I arrived here. Even better than Founder's Day." John smiled when she laughed at that. It made him feel better about leaving. "This week is going to be such a mess. You go over and over about what's going to be vacant when, and everyone agrees until you show up, and you get 'oh, I didn't know you meant this week. We scheduled meetings' The two buildings on the schedule for this week already asked if they could be done later. I'm only telling you this in case you miss me. If you need me, call. I'm in your phone under John."

Mary Margaret walked him to the door. "Don't worry about me. You won't have any time to, you'll be too busy trying to avoid Evelynne."

"Oh geez, that's right. Evelynne at six a.m. on a Monday. Wish me luck."

"You don't need luck. You need full body armor."

"Goodnight, Mary Margaret. Sweet dreams."

"Goodnight John. Make sure you eat a good breakfast. You don't want to face Evelynne on an empty stomach."

He leaned in close, and she leaned in closer until their lips met. He kissed her, soft and tender, and she returned it the same way.

"Good advice," he said and shut the door after himself. She locked up and said, "Come on, Stella. Time for bed. She shut off the lights and went to bed. It was hard to fall asleep, she kept tossing and turning. Mary Margaret felt bad for John. He was such a nice guy he should find somebody better. It really didn't matter. He'd be gone soon so the point was moot.

***

A Monday morning meeting at 6 a.m. in the summer was a joke. John knew it when they scheduled it. They needed to make adjustments and access the buildings on the new agenda. Six a.m. was chosen so the building would be empty; lecture halls would be busy later in the day. John knew if they came at 8 a.m, the building would still be deserted. They were supposed to be finished by fall, so the students weren't subject to workers crawling around their feet. He forecasted the classrooms to be finished first, and the Administration buildings last. Work was supposed to be done by October 31st. He left a two month 'buffer' period to support the new users and put out fires.

He had a field tech named Emmy who usually handled the learning curve. She knew the programs and system better than most, and she had those undefinable soft skills so useful when dealing with customers with unmet expectations. Like most people, some didn't know what they wanted until they didn't have it. Granted, it took many meetings and signatures before the job even started, and technically people got exactly what they said they wanted, but Emmy was worth her weight in gold. She could problem solve like doing a Rubik's cube in the dark, and leaving her behind for the buffer period was a wise move. He could go on to the next job and not worry about the previous one. Once they finished up this job, they would be done until the first of the year.

He was glad he assigned two techs as well as himself to attend the meeting. The university's IT people as well Evelynne and Schultz were there, so he figured it might not be a total waste. Schultz was the Operations Manager for this section. He didn't know if Schultz was his first or last name, but that's all it said on his ID, so that's what John called him. Evelynne's presence was a mystery; there was no reason for her attendance other than to be around John.

After the meeting broke up everyone headed off to their responsibilities. Everyone except Evelynne.

"John, I've been worried about you since you left Saturday. I couldn't get a hold of you and wanted to make sure you were OK." Evelynne said, standing closer than he'd like.

"Oh, Evelynne. Thank you so much for understanding about the fireworks. I hope you had a good time with your friends."

"I know how you can make it up to me. Come have a cup of coffee with me."

He looked at his watch and checked the time. He really didn't have anywhere he had to be, and he couldn't avoid her forever. "I've got a few minutes before I meet Bob, so sure. Where would you like to go?"

"We can use the break room down the hall. I just made a fresh pot." She took him by the arm and escorted him out the door and down the hall. She brought him in a small break room. It was no larger than a small kitchenette. A coffee maker on top of a dorm sized fridge, a sink, and a little round table with two chairs. Evelynne told him to sit, she'd get the coffee for him. John sat and looked out the window; the sky was overcast, much like his mood.

He wished he was having coffee with anybody else, but he wasn't. There was no way to get out of it, he had to suck it up and be pleasant. John tried to figure out what he originally found attractive about her, and the word that came to mind was 'enough.' She pretty enough, smart enough. Fun enough. No great shakes, but enough.

"John? Hello, John?" She interrupted his day dreaming. "You take your coffee black, right?" He nodded, and she nodded, pleased she remembered. He would be pleased she remembered, too. Evelynne brought him a mug, set it in front of him, and sat in the other chair, the room such a tight squeeze their knees touched. "John, did you enjoy Founder's Day?"

"Yes. It was a beautiful day to be out and about," he said as he sipped his coffee. Damn it was hot. It wouldn't be cool enough drink until lunchtime. "Pass me the cream, please."

"What's the matter, John? Something wrong with the coffee? Would you like something else?"

"No, but I got in the habit of drinking coffee house coffee, and it's so strong I started putting cream in it. Now I prefer it."

"Good to know. I missed you at the fireworks. We had such a nice afternoon it was a shame you weren't able to stay."

He nodded and sipped his coffee to avoid responding.

"What do you like to do for fun, John?"

He was so glad he had already swallowed. That question would have caused him to choke and burn his sinuses.

"Paperwork, mostly. I don't have time to get it done on site. I play in a golf league. I take a run in the park if the weather's nice."

"Golf? I've never golfed before. Would you take me sometime? I'd love to learn." She purred.

"Maybe." He said with a smile. *When pigs grow wings.*

John finished off his coffee, looked at watch, and stood. "Evelynne, a pleasure. I've gotta run now, I'm already five minutes late." He hustled out of there like a man on a mission, giving Evelynne no time to respond.

John quickly turned into a stairwell and went down two flights. He leaned against the wall to catch his breath. He decided that there can be no romantic interest between them. It's an HR issue, there were never two people alone. There could be a he said/she said situation and it's best to avoid it completely. No pairing off. No sneaking around to pair off either. That sounded good. *She should buy that,* he thought.

John avoided Evelynne. He managed to be between job sites, unavailable for lunch or coffee. Besides Emmy, the rest of his crew consisted of Bob, the senior tech, Ricky and Jimmy associate techs. Jimmy had a background in electronics. In order to get more information and useless data more juice was required.

"Hey, Boss," Ricky said. "You're on Evelynne's to-do list. She's been all over campus looking for you."

"Jesus," John said. "If she asks, tell her I left for the day. Every time. I'd don't care what time of day it is. If she gets too nosy tell, her I'm prepping the next job. I don't know what else to do. I was nice to her once, and now she's convinced I'm the 'one.' I used to wish for a woman to chase me around. No more. Believe me, it's not worth it."

"Ha Ha," Ricky said. "Maybe I'll take her off your hands for you. I wouldn't mind having her chase me around. She's not that old. She's a cougar."

"You take her off my hands for the rest job; there's a nice bonus in it for you."

***

He still ran every morning. John tried like hell to avoid thinking about Mary Margaret, but the harder he tried; the harder it was. He ran in the park and detoured by her house. Sometimes the truck was parked in the driveway, sometimes not. John liked her, he wanted to help her. He just didn't know how.

John stopped by the coffee shop a few times, looking for Casey with no luck. He couldn't figure out if he was wasting his time or not. They had such a nice time at the Bay. Then she fell apart. He tried to remember what caused her to break. They were just talking and goofing around. He asked her to be his girlfriend. *Was that it? Is that why she looked so sad?* He thought. *There's a disconnect somewhere, I'm just not getting it.*

He made himself avoid her the following weekend. John called Mark Stewart and played a lot of golf. He decided to go shopping and buy some jeans. John went to the grocery store and cooked a roast chicken with vegetables. He had done all these things by himself plenty of times. He wished he could do all these things with Mary Margaret.

John didn't know exactly why her. Maybe it was because she was a puzzle and he like solving puzzles, but she wasn't a toy to be played with. She was someone he cared about in pain. He couldn't help her if she wouldn't talk to him. *It wasn't fair to her, to make her dredge up whatever it was and spill her guts; only to say 'sorry, I have to be in Tulsa on the first.'*

John decided that if she didn't share it didn't matter. He liked her fine; she could keep her secrets. Mary Margaret was a dead end; it didn't matter what she told him. He had no ties to this place. Once his work was finished, he was off to the next job. *Best just to take a step back and leave her be,* he thought.

He was off to Target to buy new sheets. The furnished rental had linens, but he decided he needed to do something, and the only thing he could think of was replacing the sheets. They were scratchy. He stopped in the coffee shop. He stopped searching for Casey and Mary Margaret and was on his way out of the door when he heard his name being called.

"John! Over here!" He turned towards the voice. It was Casey. She sat at a table with her laptop. "Come over and have a seat."

"How are you, Casey? Still hitting the books, I see."

"I'm good, John. How are you? Seen my mom lately?"

"No, I haven't. I wasn't going to say anything, but I don't think I'll be hanging around her much anymore."

"What happened? She rip you a new one?"

"No, quite the opposite. She collapsed in a pile of tears. I confess, I was hoping to run into you and see if you had any idea why, but I decided to give your mom some space. If for whatever reason I upset her, I'll leave her be. She doesn't need any more headaches."

Casey looked at him, her mouth open. "She cried? I've never seen her cry."

"Well, I saw her. She cries."

"What happened?"

"We were just having a bite to eat, goofing around, and I asked her to be my girlfriend. You should've seen her. She turned white as a ghost and practically climbed up the walls to escape. It scared the shit out of me.

"I brought her home and she cried. She kept saying she was sorry. She cried buckets. I took Stella for walk to give her some time to compose herself. When we got back, she was okay, but I stayed a while to make sure she was going to be alright. I haven't talked to her since. I'm scared to. I can't help thinking I did something wrong. I don't want to upset her again."

"That certainly doesn't sound like her. I just saw her, and she seemed fine."

"That's why I think it's me. Nobody else makes her cry."

Casey's phone rang. She looked at the screen and said 'speak of the devil.' John stood up and said he'd be leaving. Casey pointed at his chair. "Sit." She said. "Hi Mom, what's up?

"No, Mom. I can't. Where's Jason? Oh. Camping. No, I can't. Maybe John can," she shoved phone at John. "Talk to her."

"Hello, Mary Margaret. How are you? No, I'm not busy. I was going to Target. Help? I can. I'm not busy, honest. No, the coffee shop. I can. See you in a few." He finished and handed the phone. "You know, Casey, I was avoiding her on purpose. I don't like being the reason she's so sad. It hurts even more because it seems it only happens when I'm around. Thanks a lot."

"John, I wouldn't take it so seriously. I'm sure there was something else stressing her out. It wasn't you. Go help her and see how she acts. If it happens again, it might be you. Let's see what happens today."

"Are you sure you're not going for a Psych degree? You have the talent of kicking someone in the pants and making it seem like it was their idea."

Casey laughed. "I know my mom. Crying might not be something she does on the regular, but she's human. Everybody gets to be weak once in a while. She had a moment. Let it go. Cut her some slack."

John stood up for real this time. "OK, Casey, I'll trust you. But you owe me."

She laughed. "The coffee's on me next time." He left and drove over to Mary Margaret's. She was standing in the driveway next to her truck. Her hair was up, and she was smiling.

"Hi John. It's awfully nice for you to help me. Damn that Jason. How dare he have a personal life."

"Well, he is a young guy. He's got to get it in when he can." John said. He decided not to pussy foot around Mary Margaret. *She can cry me a river, but I refuse to accept responsibility for it,* John thought. She looked at him with a puzzled look but didn't say anything.

"Here's what I need help with, you can let me know if you're interested. I have to go to pick up a few canvases, and go down to the Warehouse. I need to pour a big canvas, and I need you to help me move the paint around. You look kind of nice, maybe we should stop at your house and have you change into, well, crummy clothes. You probably don't have any, do you? We can stop at the thrift store and grab some, unless you have problem wearing other people's clothes. What do you want to do?"

"I don't really have anything at my place. When you live out of a suitcase like I do, you only bring what you need."

"How do you know what you'll need?"

He thought that was an odd thing to ask. "Everything mostly stays the same, just the locations change. I have two suits, a few dress shirts, jeans and golf shirts, some of that corporate business casual, running gear, and golf shorts. That's all. I've never been asked to do anything else. I can wear thrift store clothes for an afternoon."

"OK. Goodwill's on the way. We'll get the canvases first." She looked at him, smiled and dangled the keys. For helping me I'll let you drive."

"Deal." He thought how young and beautiful she looked, standing there in the late morning sun. He shook his head to clear his mind and focus on the task at hand. John decided he wouldn't look at her.

The first stop was the Art Supply Store. The large canvases were a special order. Mary Margaret went to the back to check if someone was in the stock room. Everyone knew her name. She even felt comfortable going past the

"Employees Only" sign. John waited outside for her. Mary Margaret came back empty handed.

"We need to go around back to the dock. They'll load them. We'll only have to get them to the studio."

"How big are these canvases we have pick them up at the loading dock?"

"Not that big. It's just easier to get them back here. It's a pain to take them out through the front door."

John drove around the back and pulled up to the loading dock. A guy and a girl placed the canvases in the back of the truck. They smiled and waved as the pulled truck away. Mary Margaret directed him to Goodwill. He parked and looked at her. She said, "let's go" and got out. John followed her in. It seemed as if she was on a first name basis with the employees there, too. She headed over to the Men's section. She looked him up and down and asked him "Large?"

She started looking at shorts. She picked out two pairs and went over to the tees. She selected two. John just followed her around until she stopped. "These should be OK. What do you think?" She held up a pair generic black sport shorts and a Tee shirt that said, 'Key West.' He agreed and asked her what the other clothes were for.

"I love these madras shorts. The navy tee matched the shorts, so if you don't want them, I'll wear them."

"They'll be way too big for you."

"So? I'll wear a belt." Mary Margaret moved towards the front of the store. She looked at dresses and picked out a very pretty sundress and headed for the cash registers. She paid and walked out. John followed behind. They got in the truck and headed to the Warehouse. His curiosity got the better of him and he had to ask.

"Why did you buy that dress? Special occasion?"

"No. I thought it was pretty, so I bought it. Maybe I'll wear it around the house."

"It is very pretty." He wanted to say 'a pretty dress for a pretty girl' but remained mute, thank God. *That sounded like a line in one of those old westerns his father loved to watch. How dumb,* he thought as he pulled the truck up to the gate. She got out and opened the lock and the gate. He pulled through and she locked the gate after him. He headed for the freight elevator, she walked there. Mary Margaret was propping the door open when he arrived. He both took both canvases and loaded them inside.

"Come on," said John. "I'll unlock the studio and you can move the truck."

She threw him the key and went and parked her truck. John headed into her studio and wandered back through the shower curtain maze. He took both canvases and set them aside. He looked at all the paint she had on a metal shelf, in so many colors. It was a rainbow. It was ROY G BIV. The space was bright; the sunlight shone through her window this time of day. He heard her come in.

"Here" she said and pitched him the bag from the thrift store. "You can drop trow behind me. I promise I won't look." She turned her back to him and grabbed bottles and equipment. There was a large piece plywood on top of a couple of sawhorses. A shower curtain acted as a drop cloth one covered the floor. Four painter props were on top of the plywood to allow the painting to dry and not end up stuck to the table.

"All set," he said.

She looked at him. "You look good, but that's not the point. Grab that jug of plain white."

She placed a canvas on top of the elevated stands. "I mixed up the colors yesterday, so let me tell you the process. 'The process.' Don't worry, a monkey could master the process. It's manipulating the paint. You mix it with some kind of bonding agent, or silicone. Those cause the bubbles. There's lots of techniques and materials, but you mix the paint with water or something sticky like glue, so each layer slides over the other and they don't mix. Each paint has its own properties, like weight. This is a commission for a client so I kind of care about the outcome. She wants it on the pinkish side, with stripes like striations. The realtor gave her my name. I have everything already mixed. You ready?"

"I'm excited. I've always been so left brained I never considered art as a hobby. I used to love to put model planes together, but still, that's pretty rigid."

"Let's mix the paints." She got several red solo cups. She showed him how to layer the paint. She showed him how to do the flip cup. She had him wait while the paint drained from the cup to the canvas.

"Now here comes the fun part." She broke the suction and paint pooled. "Watch." She took the cup and pushed away. The paint appeared all separated and swirled around.

"You do the other two." When he pushed back that art wasn't where he excelled, she said "Good. People who think what they know what they're doing ruin it for everybody else. You do that and we can start tilting. What we'll do is tilt back and forth until we like what it looks like."

"What if we don't like what it looks like?"

"That's why there's another canvas. Ready? Oh, take you shoes off. Oh, yeah, wear some gloves, too. Paint tends to travel. Pick up your end and let's go. Remember. Slowly."

They worked together to get the paint where it needed to be. To John's unpracticed eye, it didn't look like much. He watched her look at the canvas and evaluate it as she walked around.

Mary Margaret used a blow dryer to move the paint around. She took a palette knife and the white paint. She went to the larger negative space and used the white to balance out the color. She took a comb and a hairbrush and dragged it around the pour to add texture. She used a paintbrush to create the striations to mimic stone and put in some black like cracks.

"Here." She gave him the brush. "Have at it. If it doesn't work out, we can scrape it off and start over."

John gave himself over to the process. He studied and added or subtracted color depending on what balanced what, and if it was out of balance, it didn't matter. He happened to look up and saw she was smiling at him. "What?" He asked.

"Nothing. You're a natural. But you need to stop."

"Why? I thought I was doing good."

"The cardinal sin is overworking a piece. It can't come back once that happens. It's abstract on purpose. It supposed to suggest something. She wanted stone, she'll see stone. If you overwork it, it's mud. You just have to dial it back. That's the hardest part. I'm not known for my subtlety."

"I'm impressed."

"Oh, I forgot. Now we torch it to pop bubbles. You'll see cells."

"Cells?"

She lit the blow torch and began to run it over the canvas. Circles popped out of nowhere. "Cells. From the silicone, or air bubbles." She shut the torch off. She handed over to him. "Remember, righty tighty, lefty loosey. Don't get too close or hover too long. You'll burn the paint." He looked at her. "Have at it," she said.

He turned on the blowtorch and smiled. John did as he was told. He could see how it was easy it was to go nuts. Those cells popping out he found incredibly exciting. When he turned the torch off, he looked at her with this huge smile. "This is great fun. You don't have to be DaVinci to be creative."

He set the torch down and sat down on a stool over by the open window. She came over, fanning herself.

"Man, it gets hot in here." Mary Margaret said. In order to get any air, she had to stand between his legs. She leaned her elbows on the windowsill, her face out the window looking for some nonexistent breeze. John couldn't help it. She was that close he had to say something. He put his hands on her hips and turned her to face him. He left his hands there to keep her from running, but she seemed to enjoy it.

"Mary Margaret, I'm going to bring up something that's going to make you uncomfortable."

"Then why bother?"

134

"I'm confused about what happened the other day. What did I do to upset you? I want to be sure I don't do it again."

He kept his hands around her waist, her body language still loose and relaxed.

"I know I sorta crashed and burned in front of you, but it wasn't your fault." She turned and put her forehead on his shoulder. She could feel the stickiness of his sweat and smell the saltiness of his skin. "This won't make any sense to you, and it sounds so melodramatic it's cringe, but I'm not the girl for you. Find someone who is. That's not me."

"That's not fair. You don't get to decide what's the best for me. How would you like it if I decided what was right for you? You wouldn't. I know that much."

"I have serious trust issues."

"Maybe, but not with me. I'm very careful not to presume anything about you. I have tried so hard not to antagonize you. I'm not the enemy, you know. I just want to be friends. If we end up more than friends, so be it." He could feel her twist in his hands. She didn't want to consider the possibility; that was telling. John was taking to the side of her head, and she was looking out the window. She turned to face him. Her lips lined up with his.

He went in for a kiss, on impulse more than anything else. Her mouth was right there, what kind of man would pass that up? *A dead man, that's who,* he thought. John put his lips against hers, as light as a whisper. He didn't move his mouth against hers and waited for her to respond. Mary Margaret suddenly wrapped her arms around him and kissed him for all she was worth. She kissed him, she kept kissing him until the thought he might lose it and fall out of the window. He kept his hands around her waist and pressed his thumbs into the soft flesh below her hip bones, and he felt her hips lean into him. John was just as surprised when she abruptly pulled away.

"See how wrong this is?" She asked.

"No, I don't. Get back here."

"I can't. I'm not girlfriend material. I'm not even cheap fling material."

"Then what are you?"

"A three-time loser. The last one nearly did me in. There are some things that happened I can't talk about. I thought Ben was the one, and he was. Only he wasn't 'the one' for me. I dated another guy. He had small kids, and I had Casey. I knew how hard divorce was on kids and I didn't push. Maybe I should have. I didn't pry into the details of his life. Anyway, I thought I was being a supportive girlfriend. One night we go out to dinner, nothing out of the ordinary. Halfway through, he tells me he's reconciling with his wife. Once again, I how could I miss something so obvious?" She was quiet.

"The last guy I cannot talk about. He was an evil, horrible human being. Again, how could I miss the obvious? I thought once he was finally out of my life, I'd be fine. I went through therapy to exorcise him, to eradicate him from my existence. That was fine. That was good. I was fine.

"I decided I didn't want another opportunity to fuck things up, so I put my love life on ice. I've been happy for years. I took care of Casey and tried to be the best mother I could. Once she grew up, I fell into this art thing. I was happy. She had a good childhood. I did a lot of things right. I truly thought I was free from it all.

"I meet you and boom! When we started hanging out, it was cool. Then feelings developed, and for each good one, I have twenty telling me why I don't deserve it, and why you deserve better. I guess that's why I blow hot or cold. Sometimes I forget, and then reality hits me in the face like a bucket of cold water. I know you are starting to like me like that, but you shouldn't. I'm a dead end. There's nothing left."

Mary Margaret looked out the window again, avoiding his eyes. John studied her profile. She was so beautiful. How any guy could hurt her, be cruel to her; the idea of it made him crazy. He'd dump everything and marry her; and spend the rest of his life being good to her. John wished he could be so noble and give it all up for her; he had to admit to himself that was a fantasy for a younger man.

Here she was, a person of so much warmth and generosity, convinced she deserved none in return. Who was this fucker that beat Mary Margaret down so low it convinced her she was unworthy? So entrenched was her conviction that she was unacceptable she took herself out before some else has the chance to discovered it for themselves. Whatever it was ran deep, too.

John reached up and took a strand of lose hair and tucked it behind her ear. Mary Margaret looked at him and smiled. He smiled back. *As much as I want you flat on your back screaming my name, I doubt if we'll ever get there,* he thought. It's not what she needed, anyhow. Mary Margaret needed kindness, and a person with a rock-solid belief she was worthy in her corner; behind her, next to her. He could do that. John could be there for her.

"A penny for your thoughts," she said.

"Uh-huh. They're priceless." She was standing right there he couldn't help but reach out, take her in his arms and hold her tight. Mary Margaret put her arms around him and stood securely in his embrace, her face on John's shoulder. They stayed like that for a bit, but it was too hot, and they parted with a laugh. They went and checked out how the canvas was drying. He looked at it, and at her.

"What did you do?"

"I arted it up a bit."

"The painting- it looks like rose quartz and granite. The white makes you look at it, but the layers of color makes it look like stone under stucco. Your eye moves around the whole thing. It's not static. It was just like all the other ones when we stopped."

"Yeah, but remember I said 'take this brush and drag it through the paint over there? Take this spatula and put the paint on like you're covering a hole? You also asked what the glitter glue was for? Those veins there that sparkle? Good old glitter glue from the dollar store."

"I'm glad I didn't buy one of those Founder's Day paintings. I'm putting my order in now for two like this for Christmas. I want each of my boys to have one."

"A piece this size is $1200, you know."

"A bargain!" John said. "Beautiful, just beautiful. Are we almost done? It's hot in here, and not in a good way."

"Yes. Thank you for helping. It did come out really nice. Help me do your sons and you just pay for shipping. Let's go. The coffee shop downstairs has frozen lemonade. At least they used to; I hope they fixed the machine."

They drank the frozen lemonade outside in two chairs and watched as life passed by outside the fence. It mostly consisted of kids yelling at other kids and cars speeding by. John and Mary Margaret were both sweaty and gross, no different than many of the other residents on the other side of the wire. After they put their trash in the can he said, "race you back?"

"Not on your life. I'm spent. When it gets hot like this, I can't tolerate it. I mean I can tolerate it some, but not much else."

"Good. I was going to have to forfeit because there's no way I'm running anywhere. This way, I get the win, the credit, the glory and not expend one therm of energy."

"If you say so, Mr. 411."

"What?"

"4-1-1. Information. You got the 411. I got nothing."

He started her truck, and they angled the vents; the air conditioner blew full blast on them. They looked at each other and laughed. She seemed to be laughing a lot so that was positive. John walked her to the door and could sense her getting nervous. He took Stella for a quick walk. When he brought her back, he grabbed Mary Margaret, kissed her forehead goodbye and left. He watched her watch him as he pulled out of her driveway.

She smiled in spite of herself. Mary Margaret avoided the human need for connection by avoiding humanity in general. When his skin cells interacted with her skin cells, she swore she saw small sparks light upon contact. The delicate hair of her body tickled against the coarse hair of his, but it sent a thrill through both of them.

The pendulum swung back the other way after John left. She started to think about how he didn't really know her. He was familiar with Mary Margaret as a sweetheart. Sooner or later, he would discover the real her, and who she was would drive him away. Mary Margaret got depressed, and sadness filled the well made vacant by the absence of love.

Mary Margaret got up and went for a walk with Stella in the park and didn't bother to take a shower. When he held her in his arms and just let her rest there, it felt like nothing she had ever experienced. She felt warm, connected, and safe, all at the same; she was unwilling to flush it down the drain just yet.

Chapter Eight

Monday morning looked cloudy with a hint of rain. Mary Margaret took Stella for her walk earlier than usual. Summer Camp started next week and there was plenty of plans still to be made. It was decided to put the stage in the corner where the hoops were played. No hoops on Friday; replaced by live performances. It ran from noon to four. First, the spoken word and poetry readings; followed comedians and acoustic music, live bands, closing with rap performances or battles. All acts passed through Malik for approval and a time slot. Each genre brought their own audiences, so things kept rolling and no time for boredom. Too much overlap invited hostilities, so Malik was expected by the stage the whole time and acted as MC.

Mary Margaret went up to her studio before the ten o'clock start to the day of meetings. The commission piece she and John worked on together cured nicely. She brought Stella. There was no sign of Jason, meaning his girlfriend didn't get sick of him and send him home early.

He technically still lived with his mother and her douchebag husband. Jason refused to call him his stepfather, he never treated him like a son. He kept an air mattress and sleeping bag in his trunk. Sometimes he crashed there, but there was no sign of him. Mary Margaret didn't care as long as he didn't smoke pot up there. No Smoking anywhere in the building, and if caught immediately terminated. That was the fear of everyone in the Warehouse. It was an old building, and many artists used assorted materials like oil-based paint and solvents, and Mary Margaret's blowtorch, so all had a commitment to safety.

Mary Margaret brought Stella, who slept quietly under her chair. There was the final count of participants. Those studios got to pick where they wanted to set up. Many waited for a weather report before totally committing. Besides Mary Margaret, there were two sculptors, a couple photographers, The Tattoo You studio and a couple of painters. One was bringing a live model for figure drawings.

One of the issues on the table was cutting it back to one week. It was the same kids who came both weeks; it was thought consolidating it might be a better use of the studios who set up and have to break down every day. Plus, their ongoing work they delayed because they were out in the parking lot. It was easier to get donations for one week instead of two.

Maybe have the final two basketball teams play in a 'championship' game at four on the Friday. Move the stage to the opposite corner and have it only for musical acts. Use the theater for non-musical performances. If acts played during the picnic, it gave them a built-in audience of their peers and family members. The one-week camp was gaining steam. It was easier for the cops and firemen. Last year, there was a fire truck and police car available for kids to get a look inside one. There was a joke someone started, 'give the kids a chance to sit in the front seat of a police car because most of them will only ever see it from the back.'

The camp was started as a vehicle to get the community familiar with the arts and a goodwill gesture to provide a liaison between authorities like the police and firemen. The police were viewed with a good deal of skepticism by members of that particular zip code. Usually, they were ignored unless crushing it out on the basketball court or a little kid wants to turn on the siren. The committee tried to get a member of the force from that neighborhood; a young guy or girl who would give the police a non-threatening presence.

If no games were being played, they played 'horse' with the kids, or had foul shot contests. There was enough to do, but the second week last year attendance really dropped off. It was put to a vote to cut Camp back to one week and replace the second week with just the Friday cookout, and if that worked, maybe do two neighborhood cookouts a summer.

Mary Margaret wasn't happy they were talking about all these changes. She understood the need, and streamlining might not be a bad idea. Resources were finite and needed to be used carefully if they wanted a successful event. One week reduced the workload tremendously.

She knew kids came the second week out of boredom. There was nothing else to do. That was the point of it all. Mary Margaret brought that up in defense of the two-week camp; the response was this was a goodwill gesture, not a daycare.

True. The mission was to be a place to expose kids to the arts and improve community relations. It was true that could be done in one week. The Yeas won. One of the graphic artists said he could get a ten-foot sign announcing The Summer Camp would be one week, the dates of specific interests, and they gave Malik a burner phone for calls wanting to reserve a space.

The rest of meeting dealt with logistics like power cords, and who was the contact for each event. Mary Margaret was able to get the gallery to give her the space and hold an exhibition of the work from her tent. She was thinking about treating it like a traditional opening, wearing a black dress and high heels and having punch and cookies. Mary Margaret liked the idea except for the shoes. She also wasn't sure about being inside the whole time. She wanted to experience what was going on outside. Maybe if she found some kids who wanted private lessons, she could give them the exhibit opening experience; right now, it was about the outdoor activity.

There was a neighborhood contact who was on the committee and gathered together a few outreach programs from the area. There was a 'hair care' tent, a barber and his wife who had excellent braiding skills, and there was also a representative from the Gentleman's Club, a civic organization that wanted to close the skills gap between inner-city youths and their suburban counterparts.

Mary Margaret thought it was a good sign, the community taking some ownership. A pastor from the largest area church was coming. Maybe next year they'd get a dietician and a farmer's market to address the obesity epidemic and food desert. It would be nice when it got to the point where the community took it over and made it neighborhood event. Only time would tell.

***

John was in a time crunch at work. The dorms and half the campus were up and live, the improvement in speed and stability killing it. Once people got back to their offices, those yet to be upgraded called and harangued wanting to be next. Sorry. Dorms and all student housing were going online next, all office and support staff last. These kids need the most advanced information management services and bandwidth available to play 'CALL OF DUTY XX.'

Compared to what they had been using, the speed was incredible. Good news traveled fast, so the crunch was on. He met all requirements before deadlines, so there wasn't a company or supply problem. His mind was always on. John knew Mary Margaret had her big event at the Warehouse coming up; he wished he could be more supportive, but his day job was leaching into his evenings. He called and left her messages. She returned his calls with more messages.

There was a lot of work to do Monday morning before they opened the gates. Setting up for Mary Margaret mostly required labor to bring all the materials down. Jason had to make a couple trips, but Mary Margaret had consolidated a lot of items after altering the plan from the year before. From her experience, the first day started slow. Kids were hesitant, looking at all the tents but not really entering. The basketball courts started out slowly, everyone warmed up making shots.

When the attendees crossed the line from 'idle play' to 'let's smoke 'em' is when the cops versus the firemen game started in earnest. A lot of these guy were fit, as in good shape. They played a little rough to show the kids they weren't fooling. Teams started up to play the winner. Right now, it was mostly younger kids.

After lunch the older boys came around which brought the older girls. The younger kids followed their siblings until they found an item of that piqued their own interest they wandered off. She had three first grade girls come by and pour. They talked about color theory. They wanted to go again but Mary Margaret had no idea how many others would come. If they came on Wednesday and she had extra, then sure. Check back, was her advice.

The traffic to her tent gradually increased. She had Jason go upstairs and get one of the finished larger pieces along with an easel. She put that upfront, and it drew a lot of the kids in to check out how she did that, they wanted one.

Some turned their noses up at the smaller ones, but a few wanted to try. They had so much fun the girls that initially walked away came back to give it a try. A couple girls used the same colors, but layered them differently, and each tilted with their own style. They loved using the blow dryer and laughed when they blew too aggressively, and the paint splattered each other. The kids were amazed at how the paint reacted; each canvas was different.

"Now for the cool part," Mary Margaret said and pick up the blow torch. She lit it and had them each watch their canvas as she passed the blow torch over their pieces. The heat brought the silicone "cells" out and up to the surface, and colors they thought disappeared suddenly showed through.

"Wow," one of the kids said. "How'd they do that?"

"That's a question for your science teacher," Mary Margaret answered. She told them to come back Friday and pick them up after they dried. One girl was sad she would be unable to get hers; Mary Margaret promised to drop hers off. Some of the older girls didn't want to get their clothes dirty, so she asked if the younger kids wanted to do a few more with colors the bigger girls chose.

Again, the same process but different. Before they poured anything, Mary Margaret had them write their names on the back in marker. Any canvases not picked up would be held in the gallery until the end of the month, except the one she said she'd deliver.

Mary Margaret talked to the girls about inconsequential things; the vibe was peace and love, not lessons and lectures. She heard a girl scream and looked outside her tent. A boy around fifteen had a younger girl up against the fence, his forearm pressing on the girl's neck. Every time she struggled, he pressed harder, cussing her out, saying awful disrespectful things to her.

Those words echo in her head, words no woman should accept or tolerate; but most feared the repercussion if they challenged the guy. These girls had no resident father who would come out and give the guy the beat down of his life for talking like that to his little girl. There was no strong male role model to teach the boys how to grow into men, and how to treat the women in their lives. The echo got louder as her heart started to race, thoughts flew through her brain too quickly for her to focus. Her face and neck flushed red, but it was no match for the red that swam in front of her eyes. The echoes in her head solidified into one continuous scream as she left her tent.

The number the kids watched the scene but did nothing to come to the girl's aid pissed Mary Margaret off big time. They had their phones out to record any drama, but nobody moved to help. She sent one of the kids in her tent over to the half pipe to get Jason, and another to find Malik or the pastor.

She went outside and pushed her way through the crowd of kids to reach the girl in distress. It grew larger once they saw Mary Margaret about to enter the fray. She got right up next to the guy, unnoticed by him.

"HEY!" She screamed in his ear. He turned to face her, momentarily taking pressure of the girl's neck enough for her to break free. "RUN!" She yelled to the girl, and she took off. Mary Margaret addressed the crowd.

"You girls, you see this? It's never OK for a boy to place his hands on you. Run, bite, knee him in the nuts, scream as loud as you can. Do something. Tell someone. Nobody has the right to hurt you. If he chokes you out in public, what's he gonna do when he's alone with you? A guy has no right ever to touch you if you don't want him to. EVER. You girls need to stick together and help each other."

"Yo, Grandma. Go mind your business before you get hurt. What're you gonna do anyway, you old bitch?" The boy said, automatically dismissing her.

"What am I gonna do? WHAT AM I GONNA DO?" Mary Margaret yelled in his face. *Yeah, what AM I gonna do? I probably should have thought this through better, when suddenly she had the answer, the heaviness in her apron pocket.* She pulled the blowtorch out and took a step back. She looked the kid dead in the eyes and turned on the gas. She held it up and hit the ignition. The flame shot out of the front nozzle. The crowd oohed and aaahed and took a step back.

"How about I do this? How about I LIGHT YOU UP LIKE A CHRISTMAS TREE?"

He took a step back, visibly surprised she didn't back down. She took a step towards him.

"That nylon jersey is gonna go up in flames like WHOOSH and stick like glue to your burnt up skin. They'll be picking pieces of it out of your crispy fried ass with tweezers for the next ten years," she said. "How about I-"

"Mary Margaret!" Jason yelled, pushing his way through the crowd. "Stop! Stop that!" He came up next to her. "Turn that thing off! What are you doing?" She obeyed Jason but wasn't too happy about it.

"Trying to teach this kid some manners. He needs to learn you don't put your hands on anybody weaker than you. He was choking out some girl here. Some big man he is, picking on a girl. More like a coward."

"Mary Margaret, STOP!" He took the blowtorch from her. At this point, Malik and the Reverend appeared. The crowd erupted all talking at once to Malik and the Reverend. Jason pulled Mary Margaret back through the crowd and into her tent. He made her sit down and tried to talk some sense into her.

"That's what we're here *not* to do. We are supposed to be all nice and nonthreatening. Positivity, you know, not go after some kid with a blowtorch." Jason told her.

"I wasn't going to use it. Then again, he called me grandma. He called me an old bitch. I should have burned my initials in his forehead, the little punk, to teach him a lesson."

"What lesson?"

"You shouldn't call people old." She took a page out of John's playbook. "I'm not so old I can't use him for kindling."

"Double M, when did you get so angry?"

"I'm not angry, I'm mad," she said and smiled. "I saw him choking some girl who was barely a teenager, and it made me mad. I didn't go over there to set him on fire. I forgot I even had the blowtorch. I just wanted him to stop. Nobody else was doing anything. I wanted him to say he was sorry and walk away. It was only after he opened his mouth and gave me shit, I remembered I had it in my pocket."

"Well, you can't go around threatening to burn people up. There were a ton of kids with camera phones. You'll be online forever, and probably on the news tonight. You'll be branded as a racist."

"It wasn't about race at all! It was about domestic violence! It was about not being a victim! Somebody needs to teach these girls they don't have to be victims!"

"It doesn't look like that on video. They'll crop the girl out and will just be you threatening a kid with a blowtorch. Jason saw Malik and the Reverend approach. "You got company. See you later," he said as he walked away.

Malik and the Reverend came over. Mary Margaret remained seated and prepared in her head to keep a lid on her mouth. *Do not engage. Keep your mouth shut*, she told herself.

She sat silent while they reamed her out. Her behavior was unacceptable and would not be tolerated.

"Mary Margaret. We know exactly what happened. Plenty of kids recorded on their phones." Malik said. "What you did was against our mission statement."

"Did anyone show you what he did *before* I got there? Did they record the boy threatening the girl? Choking her?" Mary Margaret answered. "Of course not. If I did anything, it was to teach those young girls they don't have to be victims. They have the right to say no. They have the right to fight back, and for the record, *I* wrote the mission statement."

"With a blowtorch? No, Mary Margaret. That was wrong. Hand it over." Malik said.

"No. It's mine."

"I'll return it next week. Now give it to me."

"Jason has it." Malik was also taking away her power strip, so no more hairdryer. She caused them a lot of embarrassment. Mary Margaret's actions violated the very spirit of the program, how could they improve community relations if she were deliberately antagonistic towards the very people they were trying to reach? *God forgive me*, she thought as she opened her mouth.

"As far as the blowtorch goes, Jason has it. I'll have him bring it upstairs. He'll bring up the hair dryer, too. I don't want to accidentally give someone a bad blow out. Do you know what even happened? Why I was over there in the first place? Do you even care? I was over there because your little snowflake was assaulting a young girl; threatening to hurt her.

"I stepped up because nobody else did. What were you to doing while that kid was choking her?" *Yikes*, Mary Margaret thought. *I'm going in deep. Fuck them if they don't understand the needs of their own community.* "I am not going to let little girls grow up expecting and accepting violence from men as the norm. That domestic violence is okay, because it's not okay. Not ever. No man has the right to hit you, to lay their hands on you without your permission. If by not acting while that cretin threatened and assaulted her, I would be endorsing his behavior. He's the one that needs talking to, not me.

"I know right from wrong. I know I was right coming to the rescue of a young girl. I know I was right sending the message what that boy did was wrong. He was choking her. Did you talk to her? Do you even know which girl it was? No? I didn't think so. What message did you send her by ignoring her?

"That the guy has more value than she does, that's the message you sent her. Way to go, guys. I bet you didn't even make him apologize. He should apologize to me for calling me an old bitch. No, he should thank me. He should thank me for not torching his sorry ass."

Any goodwill she had with them she probably burned up with her last remarks, but that guy hit a nerve she didn't want to think about. She did what she did and wasn't sorry she did it; she hoped they saw it that way, too. It was done, and now she had to await her punishment. She looked from Malik to the Reverend and back again. Mary Margaret tried to keep her face blank while they meted out her punishment.

"Mary Margaret, you put us in a difficult spot here. You have been so committed to the success of this program I don't think people know what energy and effort you've put forth; but what happened today I cannot allow. It sends a bad message that you got away with threatening a black youth because you're white." The Reverend said.

"But"-

Malik cut her off. "You have be held accountable, Mary Margaret. Today is Wednesday. I think we will allow you to continue to have your studio represented, but no more art after noon tomorrow. You can be available tomorrow afternoon and Friday for kids to pick up their pictures, but you can't go to the cookout, and

148

you're no longer a member of the planning committee. You cannot be a mentor and can no longer participate in any programs. You can keep your studio, but that's it. That way, any adults who hear about it will know you were severely dealt with, and we can minimize any hard feelings the neighborhood might have towards the Warehouse. We need to preserve all the goodwill we've built up."

"Fine. Good luck with that." Mary Margaret challenged him. "You know more than half that good will was generated by me. My ideas, my friends, my contacts. I'll be your sacrificial lamb. I understand I'm an adult and I should have behaved better, and people are looking for any reason for us to fail. Just do me a favor. Don't distill this down into big bad white woman going after a poor little black boy.

"I wish when you say the blessing tomorrow, Reverend, you address the issue of domestic violence. Don't let the opportunity pass to tell those little girls they deserve better. They aren't victims, and they don't have to be. And have someone from the Gentleman's Club say something about respect. If you want respect you have to treat others with it. If it were me, I'd find a mediator and invite me and that kid on stage and demonstrate the concept of conflict resolution, but I'm out. You don't need me or my ideas. I'll pack everything up and be out by noon on Friday, and I'm done with the Mentorship Program, too. I'll keep the studio space, pay my rent and mind my own business. Let someone else save the world."

"Thanks for being so understanding, Mary Margaret. I thank you for all your efforts." The Reverend said and walked away.

"I just want you to know I fought hard for you," Malik said. "I know the little punk involved. If you lit him up I wouldn't have blamed you."

"Thanks, Malik. Maybe I expected too much. I'm not sure people know what we did to get this off the ground. I mean, every studio furnished unlimited peanut butter and jelly sandwiches, apples, bananas, bottled water, juice boxes. There was a free lunch every day all summer, no questions asked. We even had plain jelly sandwiches if a kid had a nut allergy. We tried to cover all the bases. I know I brought this on myself, but I just saw the future of that kid as a grown man beating up his wife, and none of the other kids seemed fazed by it all. To be so desensitized to it all at such a young age, well, that ain't right."

"You're a good person, Mary Margaret. One of the best I ever met. You did an awful lot for someone who had absolutely nothing to gain."

"Thanks, Malik. I'll have all the unclaimed canvases boxed up for you. I was thinking about seeing if we could use the gallery space and hanging them for a while, so kids could get like the total trajectory for something they created and all the way to finish and exhibiting it, but it's not my call to make." She spoke.

"I'll tell you a secret," Malik leaned toward her with a smile, "I think not backing down surprised the Rev. You intimidated him."

"I'll tell you a secret."

"What's that?"

"If I still had my blowtorch, I would have let him have a taste of the fear these girls live with every day."

Malik laughed. "I don't doubt it. I've got to go now. You'll be back tomorrow, right?" He said as he walked away.

Mary Margaret sat alone under her tent. Part of her was furious that kid got away with physically threatening another participant. She thought about the message sent to the girl. The boy's behavior was acceptable because he was male and she, female. She was victimized twice, once by the boy, second by the adults. All the kids who watched got the same message.

About her own behavior, she had no regrets. The boy used his size and strength against someone smaller and weaker. He could use his size and strength against her, too. The blowtorch leveled the playing field. He could have put his hands on her, but he was not going to walk away unscathed. Lost in her thoughts, Mary Margaret didn't notice the three girls who came over.

"It's Wednesday," one of them said. "You said if you had enough paint, we could do another one."

They brought Mary Margaret out of her head and back to reality. "Oh. Hello girls. I did say that, and I do have enough stuff. Let's go." She got them set up with supplies. "Make sure you put some smocks on and keep your clothes clean. The smocks were simply adult sized shirts with the sleeves cut off worn backwards. They put them on and got to work. The sound of the little girls chatting and giggling put her in a better frame of mind. This was her sole motivation for the camp; to expose this part of this world to these kids who otherwise wouldn't have any idea it existed, or if they knew about it, it was out of their reach. When they finished, they said they were ready for the fire.

"Fire? What fire?"

"You know. You turn on the fire, and it makes the bubbles pop."

"Oh, the blowtorch. I don't have it today."

"How come?"

"They took it away from me. I broke the rules."

"Are you the lady that tried to burn that boy up?"

"Yes, but no. I did not try to burn that boy up. If I wanted to burn him up, he'd be a crispy critter and I'd be in jail. See, he was being a bully. He had a girl up against the fence. She was scared and wanted him to let her go but he wouldn't. I went over and tried to break it up, but he wouldn't listen to me. Why should he? He was stronger than I was. He was stronger than the girl. What was I going to do?

"It was only then I realized I had the torch in my pocket. He seemed to like scaring girls, so I wanted to see if he liked being scared. I shouldn't have, but I lit the torch. That way, being stronger than me was no longer an advantage, so it was his turn to be scared because now I had the upper hand. Malik and the Reverend came, and it was over. I didn't have the fire anywhere near his body. I wanted him to *think* I would use the blowtorch. He may have been stronger, but I was smarter. Remember that, girls. Sometimes you have to be smarter than people.

"Also, remember what I did was wrong. You shouldn't threaten to burn people up to make a point. I can't go to the cookout on Friday, so if you want to pick up your paintings Malik will have them."

"Why won't you be at the cookout?" A little girl with braids in her hair asked. Different colored beads clicked together when she moved her head.

"I can't go. It's part of my punishment."

"That's not right," another said. "You were helping that girl."

"Not everybody sees it that way. I guess I did the right thing the wrong way. But yes, if I had to help somebody, I'd help them anyway I could and worry about the rules later. That's what I did and now I have to pay the price."

"That sucks. That's not fair." The third one said.

"Well, sweetie, if life was fair nobody would need help."

The three girls put their smocks in the pile, and on impulse one of the girls hugged Mary Margaret, and the other two joined in. The original girl said "I think you're the bravest lady ever, fire or not." The others echoed the same.

"Thank you, girls. Just remember."

"Remember what?"

"You're braver than you know and smarter than you think. Winnie the Pooh said that."

The girls giggled at advice from Winnie the Pooh and skipped off. Mary Margaret sat and felt melancholy, unable to settle in her mood because two girls came in. They looked at it and decided it was too messy. Mary Margaret offered to demonstrate how to pour, and they agreed. She didn't say too much since the girls were talking the whole time. She got in a zone, focused on the paint and tuned them out until she heard them say 'fire.' Mary Margaret realized they were trying to figure out how to talk to her about this morning, so she quickly finished up.

"Yes, that's me." Mary Margaret said. "What can I help you with?"

"Aren't you the lady who was gonna burn up Khmal?"

"Yes, but no. He was a big bully and scaring her. I wanted him to know what it was like to be scared. If I wanted to burn him up, he'd be nothing but ashes. But yes, I am that lady with the blowtorch."

"Why'd you do it? Tell him you'd set him on fire?"

"I didn't. I just wanted him to take his hands off that girl. He didn't respect my power. I had to use the torch to get his attention."

"He had to respect your power?"

"That's right."

Mary Margaret's phone dinged. It was a video of the whole incident and showed the boy choking the girl before Mary Margaret got involved. It was from Jason, who got it from one of the girls who had it on her phone. She wanted Jason to give it to Mary Margaret to prove she was defending the girl. Jason showed it to Malik and the Reverend in case they tried to spin it any way other than the truth, and he was posting it to her website in case anyone wanted to see it.

Girls came in all afternoon wanting to meet the lady who by the end of the day set Khmal on fire and burned down his house. They all left with a sense of needing to evaluate the things they took for granted in their lives.

***

Chapter Nine

Thursday morning arrived and Mary Margaret came to a few decisions.
Since no painting could be done after noon, she decided to pack up her supplies
and bring them inside. She wasn't going to go to the Warehouse Friday. Let the
kids pick up their work from Malik. Mary Margaret was convinced the whole
experiment would fail from the beginning, but that didn't stop her from trying
her hardest to prove herself wrong. The fact she put the camp in jeopardy was
not lost on her. If it failed it had a lot to do with her actions.

Mary Margaret was of the secret opinion that a bunch of do-gooders from
the suburbs would be unable to meet the needs of the inner city. They'll teach
them how to skateboard, but the kids have never seen a dentist. A pretty picture
can't help the kids feel safe playing in front of their homes. Having your family
members gunned down in front of you can't be offset by a free peanut butter
sandwich. The camp was just to give the kids a break from everyday hopelessness
that made up the daily drone of summertime in the inner city.

Maybe it was a flaw in her thinking; exposing kids to things other kids took
for granted would make a difference. Maybe some kids would believe they are
meant for better. Maybe not, but a nice diversion from the every day can't hurt.
Perhaps in the bigger scheme of things it did help. It kept them safe for a week. If
it was all they did, it was worth it. Her mind went to adding a health fair, but she
stopped herself. It wasn't her place anymore, and she had only herself to blame.

Mary Margaret got there the time she usually did on her last day. She didn't
bring anything extra down from the Godzilla Studio. If they wanted to paint,
oh well. She found it odd a group of girls were waiting for her. Mary Margaret
reconsidered not bringing down additional materials, but the girls wanted to
talk more than paint. From what she could gather, many were children who had
single moms, many needed to work more than one job to support them. Many
had grandmas raising them. They had plenty of strong female role models, but
most were so busy or too old; girls in this group grew up rootless.

They were ripe for exploitation from predatory males. Mary Margaret may be old, but she became someone they looked up to. After all, she looked out for them. She showed those girls weren't second class citizens, and they had the right to say no. They wanted Mary Margaret to teach them to be brave; how to stick up for themselves.

"I can't teach you how to be brave, sometimes you only know if you were brave afterwards. What I would do if I could, I'd talk to the police and have them teach self-defense classes after school or something. It would help you feel better about yourself if you had the skills to fight back."

"Like burn them up?" One girl asked.

"No, like sticking your thumbs into someone's eyeballs so hard you're trying to squish them back into their brains."

Up went a collective oooo.

"You know, throwing elbows isn't just for basketball players. You have to be smart because most guys are bigger and stronger. See, you guys, I'm on the shit list here. I can't do anything because of what I did yesterday."

"What did you do yesterday, Mom?"

Mary Margaret turned to see Casey. She was with Seth and two other guys. The guys were dressed to play basketball.

"Hello, Casey, Seth." She said, "If you guys came to play ball, the sign-ups are over there by the fence."

"Hello, Mrs. Welch," Seth said, and introduced his friends. He kissed Casey, said "Later, babe," and went off with his friends.

"You know why he calls you babe? So, he doesn't have to remember your name. Jason told me that."

"Very funny, Mom. How come you have all these girls around? You giving out your secret cookie recipe?"

"No." A girl said. "Because she's a badass."

"You?" Casey frowned at her mother. "You? A badass? What did you do?"

"I broke up a fight yesterday."

"With a flamethrower!" Another girl said. Casey's mouth opened but she didn't say anything.

"It was a blowtorch, Casey, not a flamethrower. Geez."

All the girls were talking and not listening. They finally addressed the elephant in the room. Casey was her daughter. She was someone's mother. The girls looked at them together and realized she wasn't exactly that old. The two of them could be sisters. The possibility that you could be a badass and not take shit from anybody and still be soft and tender surprised them.

"She's your mom? Really? Was she mean when you were little?" A girl asked.

"Yeah, she's my mom, and she was the best mom you could have. Inside she's a big softy, but on the outside she's a pit bull."

Another girl asked in a soft voice asked Casey if she was a badass.

"Of course, I am when I need to be."

"See?" Mary Margaret said, "if you're a badass all the time, you end up being a big jerk. However, if you're only a badass when the situation needs a badass, that means you're a strong person. If you're in a situation you don't think you can handle, run. No shame in being smart.

"Being smart is what makes you a badass. Also, you have the right to say no. If someone is pressuring you to do something you don't want to do, say no and leave. Get out before you need to be a badass. That's the smartest thing. Avoid the situation completely. Uh-Oh. Here comes the Reverend."

He approached Mary Margaret's tent with a frown on his face. He stomped on over. "What are you girls doing over here?" He asked the crowd.

"We're just talking." one of smaller girls spoke up. "She's teaching us about how to be smart."

Mary Margaret winked at Casey.

"Well, you girls have to leave. This activity is closed."

"Why? We aren't doing anything wrong," another girl said.

The Reverend's frown got sterner. Mary Margaret was no longer allowed to have her tent open, but the girls didn't care. Most of them had never seen a strong female take on a guy and win. The strong women they knew had a lot of their backbone beat down by life or were old like their grandmothers.

She opened their eyes that life didn't have to push you around, it was okay to push back. The Reverend didn't like Mary Margaret exerting her influence over these girls. She was a hero for sticking up for that girl. She shouldn't fill their heads with nonsense about how life could be different. That was his job.

"I'm sorry girls, but you have to run along. Mary Margaret isn't allowed to have a group in her tent after yesterday."

"But we like her. She tells us stuff nobody else bothers to," a girl said.

"I'm sorry, girls, but because of Mary Margaret's actions yesterday, she has to suffer the consequences of her behavior. Those are she isn't allowed to participate today or attend the cookout tomorrow."

"What if she was right?" One of the older girls asked. "He was hurting a girl. Mary Margaret only scared him, she didn't even touch him." A chorus of agreement echoed from the rest of the girls.

The Reverend was taken aback. He didn't anticipate the girls rushing to Mary Margaret's defense. He wanted them to understand she had to pay the price for her actions. It seemed like these girls understood and didn't care. He needed to squash this rebellion.

"Girls, what she did was wrong. She knows that. Now run along."

"No," the older girl said. "Sometimes you have to do the right thing the wrong way. God will know what's in your heart." *Way to go, grasshopper. Throw God in his face. Let him explain that.* Mary Margaret thought.

"That's enough, girls. Now go." None of the girls moved. The Reverend wasn't used to being challenged, especially by a group of girls. Mary Margaret intervened. She didn't care if the Reverend got mad at her; he already was mad. Making him madder would please her greatly, but not the expense of these girls.

"He's right. I have to suffer the consequences of my actions. And she's right. God does know what's in your heart. So, break it up, my little friends. You go have fun, but I'm no longer allowed to participate."

"Mary-" the Reverend started to say.

"Save it. We're leaving. Come on, Casey. Let's go see if your boy has any skills."

"Oh, he has skills."

"I'm talking outside of the Operating Room. Or the bedroom. I bet he operates just fine in the bedroom."

"Ew, Mom, gross. What did you do yesterday that got everybody in an uproar?"

"Nothing."

"It didn't sound like 'nothing.'"

"It wasn't that bad. Some guy had this young girl pinned up against the fence, threatening her. I went over and told him to stop, and he asked me what I was going to do about it. I wasn't sure until I realized I had the blowtorch in my pocket. I pulled it out and hit the ignition. I told him if he didn't let go of her, I'd light him up like a Christmas tree."

"Jesus, Mom." Casey laughed so hard she started to tear up. "No wonder you have groupies."

"Oh, Casey. Somebody has to show these girls they weren't born victims, and they don't have to be one. Like that stupid Reverend. 'Run along, girls.' Hell no. Why don't you man up and teach those boys how to respect women? How to respect each other?"

"Wow. Mom. I never figured you as a Normal Rae type."

158

"Not Norma Rae. She did unions. Ruth Badger Ginsburg, maybe? Gloria Steinem? Well, the road to hell is paved with good intentions. No more champion of the underdog for me. I am prohibited from attending the cookout, and my tent is shut down. I also am no longer on the board or on any committees. I am purely a tenant. I pay my rent and come and go."

"That's not so bad. Now you have time to do other things," Casey pointed out. "This place consumed a lot of you: your time, resources, and money. I know you sunk a chunk of change into this, but you always said you looked at this as an experiment. 'If two groups are polar opposite from each other, could you shorten the divide through the arts?' Last year was the first time and it was two weeks. One year out they cut it in half. Let's see what they can do without you. If they have the momentum to keep it going without you, great. It's not supposed to be a one-man job. It would be the biggest compliment in the world if they forgot your name."

"I know. I did so much behind the scenes nobody even realizes. All those grant proposals I wrote, all those donations I begged; I won't miss that. Who knows? Maybe I'll go back to work."

"Or back to school. Get a master's in art history. Knowledge for knowledge's sake. No pressure. Just pleasure."

"I could." They had reached the ball courts and watched Seth play. He looked up and caught Casey's eye. He gave her a smile and drilled a three pointer. They watched him run up and down, he barely broke a sweat. "He's good Casey, really good. And he looks like Tom Brady."

"He should be good. He played in college. I thought he looked more like John-John Kennedy."

"I can see that."

"What if he's the one, Mom? What if he leaves and I want to go with him?"

"Then you go. You were only on loan from God, honey. I knew it even if you didn't. You grew up into a great person with a huge heart. This town isn't big enough for two of us. You'll have to go; spread this goodness around."

"I don't know. We haven't really talked about anything. The future looks so far away."

"Caution. Objects are closer than they appear."

"Oh, Mom. Why should I listen to you, your expertise lies elsewhere."

"You shouldn't listen to me; I wouldn't. But he looks like a good one, Casey. Well-adjusted in a normal boy next door turned hottie kind of way. Take him over to your dad's first. They're nice and normal. It really doesn't matter. Show him you were raised by nice, loving, normal people. Squeeze me in at the end. All families have a lunatic. I'll be the crazy aunt you keep locked in the attic."

"Oh, Mom, it's true what I said to those girls. I had the best mom, at least the best mom for me. I don't want to hide you away in the attic. I'm not embarrassed my Mom isn't the traditional milk and cookies type."

"That's not true. We made cookies a lot."

"Remember you made your own cookie cutter? It was shaped like a hand grenade."

"It was supposed to be a pinecone. It was only after we frosted them green you said they looked like grenades."

"Dad said that. I didn't even know what a grenade was. We used the cheesecake pan to make stepping stones out of cement for the front bed and he got mad he'd never have cheesecake again."

"Your father. He's such a hoot." Mary Margaret said with a laugh.

They stood together and watched the basketball game. Every so often Seth would stop the game and reposition the other team. That tall guy Seth coached had improved over the course of a few games. When he blocked one of Seth's shots Seth gave him a high five. He was very good with people.

"Congratulations. In this culture of misogyny you found yourself a good man, Casey. I have to go now and pack my stuff up. I'm moving it all inside. I'm done out here. I don't want to come back tomorrow. I'm afraid if I do see the Reverend I might light him up just because."

"You want me to help?"

"No, you stay here and cheer on your boy. I packed a lot up yesterday. I'll have Jason help me if I need it. I don't keep him around just because he's pretty, you know. I make him work. I'll catch up with you later." Mary Margaret said as she walked away.

Her tent already looked empty. All the canvases left behind she already packed up in a box for Malik. The one good thing about leaving early meant no competition for the elevator or carts. She went inside and found a cart. She pushed it outside and started filling empty boxes with paint and supplies.

"Would you like some help?" A soft voice asked Mary Margaret. She was going to say no, but the voice came from one of the girls from this morning. She got the feeling the girl was reaching out to her.

"Sure. What's your name?"

"Chyrelle."

"Hello, Chyrelle. My name is Mary Margaret. The heaviest boxes Jason can bring it up."

They talked a bit while they sorted the paint into boxes. Chyrelle was fourteen and had two little brothers, or half-brothers. She never met her dad, her brothers' dad was in prison, and her mom on drugs. She was not very reliable, so the kids lived with their grandparents. Chyrelle felt bad for her grandparents being so old and chasing a couple of boys around, but they didn't seem to mind. She was glad, she loved her brothers and all, but she didn't want the responsibility of raising those boys. Chyrelle had bigger dreams.

"How are you supposed to dream big when you know they just want you to stop after high school? A lot of girls get done with school and have no idea what to do, so while they figure it out, they get stuck taking care of somebody's kids, and then they get a baby, so whatever dreams they had are over. But how do you not feel guilty for wanting what you want?"

"Some things don't always work the way you think they will. Think about it this way. Say you became a nurse? Or a hairstylist? At the end of two years,

161

you can support yourself. You can come and go as you wish. I don't think the grown-ups in your life want you stuck here. I think they would all hope you'd be different and make a good life for yourself. Anybody who doesn't want better for you only feels that way because they're stuck here themselves.

"Or, you could help at home if you need to, but because you went to school, you'd be a much bigger help. But it's your life. Live it your way. Just be careful of sweet talking boys. They suck you in and suddenly it's what they want over what you want. You have to make sure you don't fall for some smooth talker and end up with a baby of your own."

"I don't understand."

"Casey's dad. Now there was a smooth talker." Mary Margaret knew Ben would laugh at this, but she was trying to make a point. "Just keep your eye on the prize. Your mom made her choices. Now you get to make yours. They don't have to be the same. I think out of your whole school there would be at least one teacher or counselor who would love a kid that wants something more than a week in detention."

They pushed to cart over to the door with access to the freight elevator. Mary Margaret pushed the cart through the door and noticed Chyrelle standing outside.

"Come on, Chyrelle. Don't you want to come up?"

"We were told we couldn't go in this door."

"I give you permission. You can see the studio."

She looked nervous, riding in the freight elevator. The door clanged and screeched. It shuddered and she grabbed tight to the iron crossbar. It stopped the third floor and Mary Margaret opened the door. She pushed the cart as Chyrelle marveled at the old building, the shiny waxed wood floors and lots of doors. She thought the studio was the best place ever. Chyrelle looked at the exposed brick walls; at Jason's attempt as a graphic novelist.

"Wow. Imagine having a space where you can think; where the 'Price is Right' isn't blaring and no little kids are wiping snotty fingers on my jeans. Heaven."

"I'm going to give you my card. It has my email, but I'll write my number on it. Please call me if you need help. Give it to your counselor. Have her call me. I don't know if I can help. If you win an award or need a fancy dress, I can help. Only advice I have is don't do drugs and don't get pregnant. Or try the best you can. Boys are never the answer and almost always the problem. Remember that. We have to go back and get another cart full, but that should be it."

They went downstairs and back outside. Chyrelle needed to go so Mary Margaret pushed the cart back for another load. Casey and Seth were there. They went upstairs, this time for Seth to appreciate Mary Margaret's space. They finished returning her inventory and decided it was time to go. Mary Margaret grabbed a canvas and locked up. Casey said they were going over to Ben's for a cookout and invited her to go, but she told them she was tired, so after she dropped off the canvas she was going home. They walked her to her truck; Seth gave the ubiquitous manly admiration and asked to drive it sometime.

"Sure. Anytime I'm not transporting bodies from the morgue you're free to borrow it."

"That's where I've seen it before! Parked behind the hospital," Seth joked back.

"He's good, he gets my jokes and can keep up with me, Casey." Mary Margaret said. Seth smiled.

"I wouldn't be so proud of that, Seth."

"But I am. Extremely proud."

"I'll see you guys later." Mary Margaret said and pulled out of the lot. She looked at the address taped to the back of the canvas. She knew approximately where she was going and pulled up in front of a run-down brown two-family house. The paint was faded and peeled off in spots, the porch sagged. Grass grew in a few places, the rest was plain dusty, dry dirt. She put the truck in park and double checked the address.

Yes, this was the house. It looked silent. Mary Margaret figured she'd leave the bag containing the girl's canvas on the doorknob. She knocked and rang the bell, but nobody answered. She hung the bag on the doorknob and went back to her truck and drove home, to the safety and peace of mind her tax dollars bought her.

***

She went home. Mary Margaret desperately needed a shower; wash all the bullshit that was her day down the drain. She said hello to Stella and decided to sit on the deck stairs and throw the stick a bit for her. Stella was grateful and they played until dusk. Mary Margaret had not entirely absorbed what happened and what happened to her.

She's no longer affiliated with The Warehouse in any capacity other than a tenant. Mary Margaret spent a lot of her time there begging. Begging for grant money; begging for donations or help with tasks that needed doing, and now it was over. She took Stella inside and fed her dinner. Mary Margaret finally got in her shower and bawled her eyes out. *But, yeah. Wow,* she thought. *Done.*

She towel-dried her hair and wrapped herself in her thick Turkish robe. Her hair smelled of lavender and her skin like lemons. She felt like a bicycle tire that ran over a nail. Utterly depleted. Mary Margaret heard the knock on her kitchen door, she tried to pretend she wasn't home, but standing in the middle of the kitchen sort of gave it away. She looked and saw it was John and waved him in. He gifted her with a lovely bouquet of seasonal wildflowers. She tearfully accepted and put them in vase.

"How beautiful they are. Thank you." Mary Margaret said a watery voice.

"Sit down and tell me about your day," John said, and led her to the couch.

This was not the reaction he had anticipated. John expected her to return triumphant, instead she curled up on his lap like an overly large puppy. Mary Margaret tucked her head under his chin. He wrapped his arms around her. He wouldn't mind comforting her if he knew for what.

After a bit she said, "I apologize for not being better company and I'll explain in a minute; just let me have a chance to organize it all." She finally spoke and told him the whole story, ending on her ouster of any Warehouse committees and board. There was no way she could deny or defend holding a lit blowtorch amongst a crowd of children. Mary Margaret had it coming, she should have known better. Even she knew that.

"I don't know what to say. You were so involved in that place. You tried to, at least, position the place to be self-sufficient. The reason most things were successful was because of some back door favor you called in. I don't know if they realize what kind of adversary you would make if you decided not to go quietly." John said.

"I had a good cry and I'm over it. I wish them well and much success. I'm just curious what's next. Nature hates a vacuum, you know. Something will come along to fill up the space it created. We'll just have to see."

Chapter Ten

"You look clean," John said to her. "Would you be interested in getting something to eat? I was going to offer to take you out to celebrate your success, but it can be consolatory. I don't care why. I'm hungry. Would you like to have dinner?"

"Yeah. I'm hungry, too. We have to bring Stella. She's been so good this week. She deserves a night out. Let me go get dressed. Keep Stella company while you wait." He secretly said goodbye to the skin of her thigh, visible when her robe flopped open.

"Take your time. Stella and I will be just fine."

It didn't take her long to get dressed. She came out wearing the sundress they bought at the thrift store, some black sandals and a jean jacket in her hands. She looked so sunny and fresh.

"All set. I'll get Stella's leash and we can go."

"I already have it. By the way, I like your dress. It didn't impress me much on the hanger, but on you it looks stunning."

"Stunning." Her voice sounded like she didn't quite believe him. "That's quite a word for a second hand dress."

"It's the first word that came to mind. Sorry. Do you have your sunglasses? Phone? Anything else?"

"I'm all set. Let's go."

She locked up and got in his car. Stella sat on her lap, her head out window. With her sunglasses on she looked like a movie star. John was pleased she took the effort to look nice. He knew she would deny it, and say 'I just pulled it out of the closet, no big deal.'

It looked like they were on a date. John wasn't sure if she'd agree so he decided not to tell her. John called ahead and reserved a table outside. He hoped for a little bit more by way of companionship, less a therapy session, but John was grateful they were together. He had a certain fondness for her, but he was hesitant to put a label on it.

They had a drink while they waited. John went out of his way to treat her as he would an ancient relic, as if he breathed wrong, she'd crumble. She was oblivious to his predicament in the beginning; after a while she noticed.

"I'm all right, you know. What happened at the Warehouse happened, and I'm a lot better than you think. It was wearing on me, to tell you the truth. There is always turn over, and you need tenants pay the rent, so if there were vacancies, you needed to find renters. I went all over campus and craft stores advertising.

"I was more involved probably than I should have been. Time to let go. What else do I talk about? Nothing. Time to get some new material." She said. "What? Anything exciting going on with you? How's work? How's Evelynne?"

"Evelynne is now the object of affection of one of my employees. She's too wrapped up in him in worry about me. Work is progressing nicely. There's a bonus for each day we finish ahead of the deadline. Things never go as planned, but knock wood, not anything we can't handle, yet."

He sensed she wasn't in the mood to talk, so he handled the conversation. After their drink they walked to the back patio and sat at a nice table. The sun was low in the sky and bathed in the golden light she looked positively angelic. Perhaps it was the vodka martini, but John felt like she deserved to know how beautiful she looked.

"Only you could grab a dress off a sale rack at thrift store and make it look like Chanel. Maybe it's the time of day, but this light flatters you. The late afternoon sunshine illuminates you. It looks like it's coming from the inside. Like an old Master's painting. It looks like you glow."

Mary Margaret gave a little giggle and blushed. "I'm sure it agrees with most women here."

"No." He insisted. "It's not. It's you. You're beautiful."

She laughed again. "Have another drink and I'll look like Marilyn Monroe."

"No. You have another drink. I want to look like Brad Pitt."

"I might need the whole bottle for that."

"Have two bottles, then." He ordered another round. The waitress took their dinner ordered and left, a promise to bring their drinks right back. She delivered the drinks and left. They each took a sip and looked at each other. He had this huge grin on his face.

"What is wrong with you?" she asked.

"Nothing. Everything. I get around you I lose my place in the universe."

"You're not making sense."

"I can't. When I look at you, I forget everything and start babbling. I'm humbled by your beauty."

"Stop now or I'll call an Uber."

"You're no fun. I'm trying to cheer you up."

"You don't need to cheer me up; I'm fine. I'm sure I'll notice it more next week when I have nothing to do in my spare time. Otherwise, I'm looking forward to finding a new hobby."

"You could do me. You could be my girlfriend."

Mary Margaret swallowed the wrong way and started to choke. John jumped up and pounded on her back until she stopped coughing. "What is wrong with you and this girlfriend shit? I'm sorry, but that's out of the question."

John sat back and gave her an appraising look. "I only say that because it gets such rise out of you. I didn't mean for you to drown. Don't worry; I'll drop it. Someday maybe you'll tell me why whenever I mention it the color runs out of your face and your eyes search for the exits."

"That's it," she said, and pushed her chair back. "Take me home."

"No. Our dinner will be out momentarily. I won't bring up again. I shouldn't tease you if it upsets you so. I can't help it if we get along. I make you laugh, you make me laugh. I can't help it if sometimes my imagination comes out of my mouth, and when the sunlight hits you just right, well, it doesn't matter. Oh, look. Our food. Let's eat and forget this nonsense."

"Do you promise not to bring it up again? Can't we just have a nice dinner and forget about everything? Just enjoy a nice summer evening?"

"Yes. I won't say anything else. It is a gorgeous day. Except I'd sit across from you in a hurricane and still enjoy it."

"John."

"Mary Margaret. That steak looks delicious. I hope it tastes as good as it looks."

"It does. Now it's time for me to eat. That camp takes a lot of you. Being a goodwill ambassador from the suburbs is hard work. Now I can be like everybody else; write a check and be done with it. I can feel good about myself and not leave the house."

"Yes, be like all the other philanthropists. Care all the way to your yacht and sail away without a guilty conscience."

"It may only be a rowboat, but it's the same sentiment."

"How's your dinner?" John asked.

"Delicious. I can't believe I'm going to finish this; I'm that hungry. I'm sorry, Stella. No doggie bag for you."

"She won't mind. I've been slipping her some scraps under the table. Stella won't have room for dessert. How about you? Want something sweet?"

"I saw chocolate cake on the menu. I love chocolate cake." She confessed.

"Chocolate Cake it is." He waved the server over and ordered a piece of cake for Mary Margaret.

She took a bite and said "Yum. Take a bite." He did.

"That is some good chocolate cake," he agreed.

They sat there after dessert, smiling and sated. Mary Margaret smiled at John. He smiled back. "Feeling better? I hear chocolate releases chemicals in your brain that make whomever you're dining with look like Brad Pitt."

"Are you sure it's not the booze?"

"You're probably right, but chocolate sounds better."

"Why do you do this? Hang around me, I mean. It's a zero-sum gain. There's no point to this." Mary Margaret asked him, curious about his answer.

"Maybe that's why you did what you did at the Warehouse. You knew you were ultimately going to fail, but you did it anyway. You know, throw it against the wall and see what sticks. I don't know very many people. I guess that's because my job is all over the place, I have a storage locker with some things, mostly their grandparents' things for the boys. Who knows what's in there? Maybe they can have it on the that auction show. It's outside of Philly. I pay for it a year ahead. That's about all I think about it; once a year." He looked at Mary Margaret.

"You know, the answer to your question is I like you, that's about it. I go to the store, the dry cleaners, the coffee place, I even went to Founder's Day. What a meat market," he joked. "I try to get familiar when I'm in a new place, get the lay of the land, and I look. I look at people and it's like looking at a bag of apples. They all look the same, more or less.

"Then one day I buy a bag of apples. I get home and open the bag because I want an apple, and I pull out a peach. A soft, ripe, juicy peach. So juicy it runs down my arm faster than I can chase it with my tongue. After that peach, who wants an apple? A man will spend the rest of his life searching for another peach like that."

"Are you saying I'm the peach or the apple?"

170

"You pick. I've only heard tales of such peaches. I've come across a few, but it's like Goldilocks. This peach is too hard, or too ripe. I've never found one just right."

"Those peaches aren't true. The outside looks good. That usually means there's worm near the pit."

"Is that what's wrong with you? A worm at your core?"

Instead of getting up and having a snit she sat there and answered him. "Something like that."

"Whatever you think you are, you'll become. It can't be that bad. What, did you kill someone? They probably had it coming," John told her.

"Those are some nice sentiments, but untrue. Some things are just facts. Not much you can do about those," said Mary Margaret. "Just because it happened a long time ago doesn't change today."

John stayed silent. Finally. She trusted him enough not to deny there was something, even if she didn't tell him what it was. Whatever it was, it was strong enough to bother her years later. What would he do if she confessed to human trafficking or being drunk behind the wheel and taking out a family of five? She was a serial killer? Harvested babies to sell placenta on the dark web? It bothered her, whatever it was. She parted the curtain. It was still too dark to see, but now there was a sliver of hope.

"I don't want to know. As far as I'm concerned, you fell out of the sky yesterday. I hope you enjoyed dinner. I know I did. Stella, not so much. Why don't we stop and walk her in the park? It's still a beautiful evening."

"I think it's a nice night. I bet she'd love a walk." He drove the short distance to the park and they started out on a path. They went slow and let Stella's sense of smell guide them. He managed to grab her hand and she didn't pull it away. She seemed to be used to holding his hand. *So Mary Margaret has a secret,* he thought. *What it is, I don't care. Let her keep her secrets.*

After a while they sat on a bench and let Stella wander around untethered a bit. He was still holding her hand. Suddenly, she pulled her hand back and used it along with her other hand to cover face and let out a huge sob. Stunned, he put his arm around her. He made small soothing sounds and rubbed her back.

"Oh, God, John, what did I do? I lit a blowtorch and threatened some kid with it. Why did I do that? Why?" She sobbed in his arms. "I know why. It was the only way to get his attention. It was so extreme. He was choking some girl and one of the rules is we don't touch any of the kids. I had to light it. I didn't think about the other kids. They actually thought it was cool. The mission was peace and love. I fucked it up big time. I told him I'd light him up like the Fourth of July. She is wrong with me?"

He wasn't surprised she reacted like this. John was surprised she hadn't broken down sooner. He knew she loved that place, as much as she tried to say otherwise. It gave her a purpose. It gave her an identity. John was surprised she lit the torch, but not really. He imagined she'd make a great Joan 'd Arc, swinging her broadsword, mowing down the Moors. Or was it nonbelievers? Unruly Frenchmen?

She was strong, no shrinking violet, her. And impulsive. And sexy. John hadn't really had the hots for a woman in years. He was glad. It was a lot of work, the whole romancing a woman and then having to keep her happy. To John, it was a young man's game. Let them bang their heads against the wall hoping they'd done enough to get laid, and now look at him. He was willing to bang his head against a wall for her just to make out with him.

She sat back up and wiped her eyes with hem of her dress. "Sorry. I don't know what came over me."

"It's not too hard to figure out, Mary Margaret. We like to think since we've been around a while, we are blessed with some smarts along with our AARP card. I think as you get older you don't get any smarter, it's now you take less risks. You don't need to, a lot of choices have already made, like school and family; things like that. The essence of who you are never changes, it's the ability to execute that changes. You get tired after a while.

"I haven't known you that long, but I feel like I've known you forever. You are a person with a big heart who isn't afraid to challenge the status quo. I look at

Casey, and even Jason. The Warehouse. You love hard, Mary Margaret. There's no sin in that. The problem is most people can't keep up."

"The Warehouse meant something to you. As much as you say you're glad you're finished, you're not. What happened wasn't your choice, you didn't decide it was time to go. You got shown the door. You got fired. Your service is no longer required. It's OK to hurt. It's grief, Mary Margaret. Plain and simple. You lost something you loved. Be sad. Cry on my shoulder. If you deny it, it's only going to hurt longer."

"That's true. I feel like I lost an arm or something. I didn't realize how consumed I was by the place," she said, and snuggled next to him. She put her head on his shoulder. "For not knowing me, you did alright."

"I'd like to think I'm some sort of genius, but I'm not. I'm human. You're human. Life has its challenges. Anybody who thinks they're immune is delusional. I think the key to happiness is finding someone with whom you share mutual delusions." He leaned in closer. "Care to indulge in a delusion with me?" Mary Margaret leaned in and put her mouth on his. "Uh-huh." She said and kissed him. He put his hand on her neck, his thumb stroking the tender spot by her earlobe he found so fascinating before and kissed her back.

"Oh," she said.

"Oh what?"

"You know how I got bounced because I lit the torch? I don't think I told you the whole story. Yes, I went over to help the girl. I sent someone for Malik. I planned on distracting the kid until Malik came. I didn't light it because he called me a bitch. I lit it because he called me OLD. Who did that little shit think he was, calling me old? I figure you'd find that funny."

"In a painful way, funny."

"Not really."

"No, we're not old."

"No we're not. Is this considered mutual delusion?" Mary Margaret asked.

"I don't know what the criteria is, but I'll indulge it as a mutual delusion if you will."

"Sure. Let's." She said as she laughed, her head still on his shoulder. After a bit they got Stella and headed to the car, still hand in hand. He drove his car and parked in her driveway. He got out to walk her to the door. He didn't want to kiss her; that wasn't quite true. He did want to kiss her, but needed to get her in his arms first. Move too fast and she'd bolt.

"I'm not going to ask to kiss you, I already know the answer. How about a hug?"

"That I can do." She said she stepped in his arms and enveloped him in her embrace. John hugged her; he felt her body and was mad he only had two arms. He wished he was Hindu and made up of arms. John wanted to enclose her like a cocoon; have every inch of her touch every inch of him. He reluctantly let go, but not until he kissed the top of her head.

"Thank you, John. You're exactly right about the Warehouse. It hurts to be uninvited from all those things I used to do. I have only studio space now, but the Godzilla Studio lives on. Thanks for pretending to be old with me."

"There is nobody I'd rather pretend to be old with. Have good night Mary Margaret. You too, Stella." He made sure she was locked in and signaled her to put the door down. She waved to him from the front window. John was pleased. He watched get safely inside. She watched him safely leave. That was enough for now.

Chapter Eleven

Mary Margaret had no upcoming shows. During this lull, she started to knock them out in order for them to dry in time for the two shows she always did around the holidays. She would break for the holidays and then start creating inventory for the spring and summer shows. Mary Margaret only did four shows a year, listed on her web page. She also listed those pieces for sale and her Email address for commissions.

That's where Jason came in. He designed and monitored her website and wanted her to expand into all areas of social media, but she didn't care. Mary Margaret wasn't out to be rich or well known, she liked the creative process for the mental stimulation. She sold them to make room for more. The realtors wanted the most dramatic pieces, the larger the better, but finding room to dry them was a problem. Those were her favorites. Summer was just about over and time to change her focus on creating inventory.

Ben and Sheila hosted an annual Labor Day party. Casey was going and bringing Seth. Ben invited Mary Margaret with a guest, usually it was Jason. She brought Jason so he could secretly lust after Casey. This year, though, since Seth was around, she wasn't sure about bringing Jason. She needn't worry, Jason was going camping again and wasn't going to be around. She decided to bring John since he didn't have anywhere to go. Mary Margaret made her special Mac and Cheese, John brought cases of beer and soda.

When they arrived, the party was in full swing. Seth fit right in. He played basketball with Casey's not so little anymore brothers. They were excited to have a guy hang around. Ben played with them, but Seth was a lot younger and actually played with them. They thought he was 'cool.' He could ball.

Ben was glad Mary Margaret brought John. She was still his best friend after Sheila, and he was very overprotective of her. He used Casey to keep tabs on her. Not to spy, but to make sure being alone didn't make Mary Margaret a target of men with suspicious motives. After meeting John and watching the way he looked after his ex wife; Ben was satisfied that John acceptable and relaxed.

Sheila was the consummate hostess. Mary Margaret laughed and told her she must have Martha Stewart on speed dial. Sheila even went as far as having water balloons hidden around her house for when the youngsters got bored or too hot. Kids looked around to find the locations of the hidden balloons for when the signal was given for the start: Ben tossed the first ballon and then it was game on. Sheila had coolers in the garage filled with balloons. She had buckets of water balloons all over her yard hidden in the bushes. She even had them in her mailbox.

Mary Margaret saw John and Ben off to the side, talking like old friends. She went over to see what they were talking about. She presumed it was her since they had nothing else in common.

"Alright, you guys, spill it. What's so interesting, and you better not say me."

"That's some ego you got there, Marym. Why would you bother thinking we'd want to talk about you?" Ben teased.

"Yeah," John agreed. "He's giving me the name of his bookie."

"Yeah, right. That's a lie right there. He's too cheap to gamble."

"His dry cleaner? His therapist?"

"What your intentions are towards me?" Said Mary Margaret.

"What's the point in that? We all know how you feel about me. You want me to keep coming around and embarrassing myself?"

"Are they noble? Your intentions?"

"Not on your life. I can't be trusted."

"Well, hey," said Ben. "Looks like I'm not needed here anymore." He walked away. Neither one noticed. She brought up the topic of his job. He told a few that he was glad he dodged Evelynne's stories.

"Does it have an end date?

176

"October 31st. Still right on schedule. If I get an invite I might stay through Thanksgiving, but I need to prepare for Tulsa in January."

"I need to finagle an invite, too. I'm wondering if Casey would like to host Thanksgiving. She can showcase her cooking skills for Seth. You're welcome to come, John. It's probably written down somewhere it's rude to invite guests to someone else's party, but Emily Post doesn't live here."

"It might be, but I like to cook. Maybe she'll let me do the sides."

"I can do the pies."

"What about Ben? What can he do?"

"The dishes."

***

Chapter Twelve

Mary Margaret used September to work on her pieces. She saw Malik a few times. He was very nice, he felt terrible about how she was treated and was already missed. She told him she understood and brought it on herself.

"I'm going to miss you guys, too."

"To tell you the truth I'm not sure how we'll do without you."

"You'll be just fine. I doubt you'll even miss me."

She had a few realtor requests for staging pieces. Jason came in to help Mary Margaret. He asked her if she knew what she needed help with in October. She only had two she could think of, and he wanted to know if they could do them next.

"We can, but what's the hurry?"

"I don't know how to say this double M, but Brett and I are moving to Denver. It won't be until the middle of October. There's not much happening here, so we're going to go visit Ronnie and check it out. Who's gonna help you? I'll get as much done as I can, but what are you going to do?"

"I don't think I'll ever be able to replace you, Jase. Maybe the new guy I hire to do my lawn. Or maybe offer an unpaid internship through the Art School. I'm sure going to miss you, though. You're one of my only friends. Now that's sad. I have no friends my own age. I'll have to go down to the senior center and learn how to plan Bingo."

"I've played poker with you. You can go down there and hustle some unsuspecting old guys out of their pensions. But really, double M, you are my friend. I will miss you. Maybe you're only thing I'll miss. I'll probably miss my mom and her kids, but overall, everyone else I know has left."

"Of course you have to go. Go. You can always come back. This place will always be here. I'll find someone to help, but I am really going to miss you. Maybe I'll come see you out west. I'll do a show or two."

"I hope you do. I want you to. In the meantime, I'll help you get as much inventory as possible."

"I could build up enough inventory if only I could figure out a better system to dry them."

***

A few days later John called. He wondered if he could borrow her truck, he had something he needed to move. She said sure. People always told Mary Margaret she was too trusting. She didn't ask what he wanted it for, or when he'll bring it back. When faced with such questions her answer was 'I'm not sure.' It was her nature to believe in the best of everybody.

Even in high school, she'd loan her class notes to anyone who wanted them. She would be running around like mad trying to find whoever had them before class. Even after she got burned a few times she still loaned them out. She learned enough to make a copy of them in the Media Room and give those out, protecting her originals.

John borrowed her truck and had it for a few hours when Jason showed up. He wanted her to come down to the Warehouse with him. Jason said he had a surprise for her, so she got in his car. His car was older and smelled like gas and oil. He even had grass seed that spilled out of the bag and onto the floor in the back seat. It had started to sprout. Mary Margaret commented on it.

"Jason, I think you need to clean the back seat, or at least mow it."

"I know. I keep it like that on purpose, so nobody ever wants to ride with me. Since I'm leaving, do you want it? You know, like you bought the truck?"

"I know my car is old, Jason, but it's in way better shape than this piece of shit. Maybe I'll give you five hundred for it if you promise to have it towed to the junk yard."

"You'd do that? Give me five hundred for it?"

"Yes, I would. Consider it a bonus. You've been a great help to me, and I feel lucky and blessed to have you around. You have to get rid of it, though. I don't want this thing parked in my driveway."

They pulled into the Warehouse parking lot and parked next to the freight elevator in the back. Her truck was already there.

"That's my truck. What's John doing here?"

"It's a surprise." He looked at Mary Margaret. He knew how she felt about surprises. "Don't worry. It's a good one." They rode the elevator to their floor and entered the Godzilla Studio. John was already there.

"Hi John. What's going on? What are you doing here?"

"Come here. Look what Jason made you."

She walked over. There were two tall bookshelves with the backs removed flat against the wall. They had been spray-painted with graffiti.

"Bookcases? Thanks, but what are they for?"

"Just watch." Jason went over next to John. The two of them pulled the bookcases away from the wall and placed them so they faced each other. Jason took a large canvas and placed it on a shelf; John took the other end and placed it on the opposite shelf of the other bookcase, the canvas suspended between them.

"It's a drying shelf. You can move them closer together or further apart depending on the size." John took some yardsticks and placed them on other shelves.

"You can use these to put other smaller canvases on at the same time. You can adjust the width by just moving the yard sticks."

"Oh, my." Mary Margaret said. "This is going to work out perfectly. Thank you." *How sweet of Jason to figure out how he could replace himself,* she thought.

"Thank John. He found them out on a curb. Can you believe someone was throwing these out?"

"Wow. John. I converted you into a garbage picker. I'm sorry, but thanks, this is perfect. I can push them against the wall when I'm not using them. Thanks, you guys." Mary Margaret's voice trembled. "John," she stopped.

She couldn't get any more words out or the tears would fall. "This is unbelievable. You picked these out of the trash for me. That's so sweet." She bawled.

Jason could sense an emotional tsunami about to break, and he was leaving because he was sure it didn't involve him. He left; she could get a ride home with John. *They could have their emotional moment to themselves,* Jason thought.

"Mary Margaret, it's not like I cured cancer. I pulled some bookshelves out of trash and had Jason Art them up. He feels awful about leaving you."

"No, I think he's nervous about leaving it all. I'm a small part. Our little boy is growing up, and it's the way it's supposed to be. He should be looking forward, not back. He's a young guy. He's leaving his parents, his friends, all his girlfriends, the Warehouse. Life without a net, you know. He has friends out there, so it won't be like he's starting completely cold."

"He was asking me a lot about what I do. I think he's interested in computers. I gave him the name of a guy I know from college. Maybe if he leaves, he can better listen to his inner voice about a career. It's too noisy here, and what I mean by noise; I mean the girls, the Warehouse, Godzilla Studio. His focus was split all over, I think he'll do fine once he settles down."

"He talked to you? He's good with computers. He manages my social media presence."

"Yes. When were working on the shelves we talked. He's a nice kid. I think once he saw Casey's boyfriend was no slouch, he decided she was a dream that was never going to come true. Now he doesn't have any reason not to go."

"Was he that stuck on Casey? I thought that was a teenage crush."

"Hey, don't minimize his feelings. They aren't any less painful because he's not a girl."

"It's not that. I guess if you're gonna dream, dream big. Casey was so much older than him I didn't think he was serious about her."

"Maybe that was the attraction. He could crush on her all he wanted, she would never reciprocate, thereby shielding him from heartbreak. He's growing up a bit and willing to take some risks."

"Oh, I wish him only the best. He's a nice guy and a super sweet kid."

"He thinks the world of you. Now you aren't involved in the Warehouse, neither is he. It's not the same and he thinks it's a good time to make a change. Everything you did there he was your shadow. He thought you took on too much, now it's not a worry for him."

"I didn't know he felt like that. He wasn't supposed to feel responsible for me."

"He didn't feel responsible for you, he cared about you. You gave him a place to go when some of his friends were using drugs. He had a place to go when he needed to hide out. And you gave him his art space. That was a dream he never had to give up, and it saved him from running the streets. He never felt stuck, he felt supported. You had his back. Now it's on him, but I think he's up for it."

"I think so, too. He's grown up. He's not some kid. He's a man. Too bad he's leaving so soon. You could have given him manly lessons." She paused. "What good would that do? You're leaving, too."

John chose to ignore the last part. "Yes. You should be very proud. You raised a nice young man."

"Not me. His parents."

"You two never talked about his home life? From what he said to me his stepfather threw him out. His mom finally got him back inside, only he had to sleep on some moldy old sofa in the basement. Not a finished basement, but exposed heating ducts and pipes. So, he was clean and dry but not much else. You filled a need for him at a time when he had one."

"You're going to make me cry. He's probably my only friend and he's leaving. I'm not sorry for him, I'm sorry for me. I told him I'd come out to Denver. Yes. In the spring, when the desert's in bloom. We'll fly into Phoenix, drive through the desert and go to Denver."

"Are you inviting me to go with you?"

"I guess I just did. Sorry. I was just thinking out loud. Who knows where everyone will be by the time, I get around to it? You're going to be in Tulsa, and off to somewhere else. I don't even know how far Phoenix is from Denver. I just heard that the desert in the spring is filled with blooming plants, and I always wanted to see it. Put it on the bucket list, I suppose."

John didn't say anything. It was the first time she ever spoke about a future and him in the same sentence; he didn't want to jinx it by asking questions.

She returned to the bookshelves. Mary Margaret ran her hands over them. Jason spray painted Godzilla on the sides. She wondered if these bookshelves symbolized her life. Empty, with no back to keep things from falling off, but the decorated sides made it look interesting. That was her. Something no longer of value but repositioned for another use.

"I can't tell you how happy you guys made this for me- a drying rack that can hold a lot canvases. It's perfect." Mary Margaret turned to John and went to kiss his cheek but missed and the kiss landed on his mouth. It lasted but a second but stayed in John's mind for the rest of the day. Her lips were so soft and warm. He wished he knew what she was going to do that so he had a chance to return the kiss. Instead, he felt like a moron standing there with his dick in his hand.

"I'm glad it makes you happy. I found them and called Jason to meet me and bring some rope. Some lady pulled up and got out of her car. She wanted them and wouldn't accept the fact I saw them first. I didn't know garbage picking could be so dangerous. Good thing Jason showed up when he did. I thought she was going to fight me for them."

"You're right. When it comes to free stuff on the curb, all bets are off. Haven't you ever watched 'Hoarders?' Well, thank you for risking life and limb to get them. They're perfect," Mary Margaret said, and this time he was ready for it when she leaned into him to give him a kiss. He kissed her back with a hunger he never felt before like she was a woman who was like no other woman in the world. Her lips caught his hunger and she leaned into it further. They broke apart as the heat they were generating was going to set their clothes on fire.

"Whew." Mary Margaret said, fanning her face with her hand. "Remind me not to kiss you anymore. I feel like I'm going to faint."

"Really? Let's kiss some more and see what happens next."

"Maybe later?"

"Anything for you," he said as her caught her eye and smiled. She smiled back.

"You know how I only do a few shows a year? It won't take near as long to make enough inventory. No more Warehouse, the creative process distilled down to only what's necessary; I think I need a new hobby."

"Don't do that. Take a few years off. Go see Jason. Maybe just look around and see things. See things with fresh eyes. Maybe you want to winter on Arizona and start watercolors of cacti."

"Sounds nice, but I'll probably just end up here. Here is good. Casey's here." Mary Margaret said. She walked over and hugged John. He quickly hugged her back.

"Here is good." He agreed. He loved the smell of her shampoo. It was lavender. He went so far as to look in her shower and check out her hair care products. Lavender shampoo and cream rinse. They went over to the window. He sat on the stool and she stood between his legs like last time; her elbows on the sill and her face out the window, hoping for a fresh breeze.

Mary Margaret brought herself in and faced him. He put his hands on her hips and pulled her close. John put his chin on her shoulder and just enjoyed the feel of her in his arms. He wanted to stay there forever, but he had a few other things he wanted as well. He wanted a lot of things, but what he wanted first were some answers. John turned her around, so the back of her head was in his face. He tightened his grip on her and spoke.

"Mary Margaret. I'm going to ask a few questions." He felt her stiffen. "Yes or no questions. You don't have answer. Just say pass."

"Ah, I guess so. But not too many."

"Deal. Do you have fun when you're with me?"

"Yes."

"Do you kinda like me, even just a little bit?"

"Yes."

"Are you scared of liking me?"

"Yes."

"Are you afraid of what liking you might mean?"

"Yes."

"What are you afraid of?"

"Pass."

"Will you ever tell me what's the matter?"

"No, because it doesn't matter. End of October and you leave."

"But it's not me, is it? Do I have bad breath? Bad manners? Am I rude or obnoxious? Do I embarrass you in front of your friends or family?"

"No. You seem very popular. Everyone likes you, too. It's not you."

"That leaves you."

"Yes. I have some dark and twisted issues three years therapy didn't resolve. I'm stuck with them. I refuse to spread the misery around. It's mine, I own it, and nobody else has to pay. I've said more to you than I ever have to anybody else, not even Ben."

He watched the walls she erected close her off, and the mask settled over her face.

John smiled at her. She gave away more of herself than she wanted and although it didn't tell him much, it told him it wasn't him.

"Come here and shut up," John said and turned her around. "I'm sick of the sound of your voice. You talk too much." He grabbed her and held her tight. Mary Margaret didn't put up struggle and leaned into him with a sigh. He sighed back and held her tight in his embrace. They stayed like that for a bit, until Stella cried at being excluded. They left the Warehouse and headed off to get an ice-cold drink.

***

It was heading into a warm fall. They had fans at Godzilla Studios to move the air around only to have the windows closed and sweaters needed the next week. Jason was at a loss what to do with his antique drawing table. He was bereft of it going to someone who wouldn't respect its quirks, the nuance of such a fine table. Mary Margaret said he could store it in her extra upstairs bonus room if he could get it up there. He was extremely grateful when he met Seth on a Saturday morning to help move it. That made it real. His studio broken down hit him hard.

She still was working Mary Margaret was in a zone. Jason only hung out once or twice with her; he found himself uncomfortable sitting where he'd soon be leaving big chunk of himself. He thought about the things he'd miss doing and the list was short. Jason was stoked to be heading out west with his bros. He was looking forward to the newness of something. Anything. He exhausted pretty much anything of interest here years ago.

It was just the studio, and Mary Margaret. That's what he couldn't say goodbye to, her. She sent a text saying make sure to shoot me an email if you get bored. She'd follow him on Instagram to watch his adventures. Mary Margaret told him she loved him, and he'd always have a place at her house. He came by the Sunday before he left and hugged her goodbye. She said all she needed say in the text, so the mood was upbeat and optimistic. He left the week before Halloween.

After Jason left Mary Margaret was surprised at how much she missed him. She wasn't aware that he had become more than her assistant, or protege in the time he spent with her. He helped her so much when she took the space at the Warehouse. He expressed how lucky she was to be able to have a space like this. He didn't have to listen to the washer or dryer, or his mom yelling at his brothers and sister while trying to create something. His younger siblings were the natural children of his mom and stepdad. He knew he looked just like his bio dad the older he got, something that reminded his stepdad of his mother's 'mistake.' She dropped out of college to have him, and by his first birthday his biological dad dropped out, too. He just up and left one day.

His mother moved into his grandparent's house so she could finish college. His grandparents were kind and loving; he barely missed not having a father. They supported him and loved him as best they could. Even if Gramps arthritis made playing catch not very challenging, his grandparents showed up to every one of his games. He was very happy growing up with his grandparents, but he felt left out when his mom married his stepdad Steve and they all moved in together. Jason knew his mother loved him. She took every opportunity to express it with thought or deed, but once she married Steve things changed.

It was almost as if she loved him as much as Steve would let her. Jason was a symbol of his wife's past mistake, his stepdad's word. Jason was around ten years old, and not stupid. Jason's self-esteem took a hit. Him? A mistake? Why had nobody ever told him that before? As he aged into his teen years his stepfather treated him worse by the day. Jason had a half-brother and sister by now, and his mother was stretched very thin, trying and failing to keep a harmonious home.

Steve blamed Jason. Jason was tall and youthful, handsome; full of life and hormones. Whether Steve admitted it or not, he didn't like Jason as a kid, and as he turned from a boy to man he liked him even less. As Jason grew up his stepdad grew as well. Only Steve grew older, heavier and bald; Jason reminded Steve of his lost youth and vitality every time he saw him. The clashes got more frequent. Jason's mere presence set Steve off. It upset Jason, seeing his mother cry because of her inability to create peace between them. He hated Steve for making his mother choose between them, so he spared her the guilt and chose for her. He ended up back at his grandparents.

His grandparents aged since he left. He thought it great at the time, answering only to a couple of old people. He had no curfew or supervision. When he was sixteen, he got busted for possession. His friends passed a hat at school to raise his bail money. Because of his age his mother was called. He wasn't allowed to leave unless in the custody of a parent, so his mom came and brought Steve. His friends were in the parking lot waiting to give him a ride.

Steve started in on him as soon as they hit fresh air. He listened to Steve go off about what a disappointment he was to his mother, as well as the many reasons he was a failure. An embarrassment to the family. A loser. Jason usually avoided confrontations with Steve since he knew how much it upset his mom, but his mom did nothing but cry. She never once up stuck for him or told Steve to stop. She never would, either. That was the reality of the situation. The only person who was in his corner was him, and he could either fight back or lay down and take it. Jason had enough and looked at his stepfather.

"Why don't you shut the fuck up, you fat little prick," he said. He stepdad took a swing at him, and for the first time Jason swung back. He connected with his stepfather's nose. He heard a crack and blood gushed out. His stepfather started screaming. They were in the parking lot of the police station and there were officers around.

"Arrest him! He assaulted me! Arrest him! I'm bleeding!" Steve yelled to some nearby officers.

Jason watched as the cops approached his stepdad. He didn't bother to get in his friend's car. He figured they were going to cuff him and bring him inside; he'd save them the trouble of a high-speed chase. It would end up back here anyway. Jason wondered why he couldn't catch a break, why the adults in his life consistently failed him. Here he was, almost an adult himself, and starting to feel like the big fuck up he'd always been accused of being. How could anybody expect him to be more when that's all he ever heard? Then something happened that offered Jason hope. It was only a single strand, but it was enough for him to hang on until something offered him a firmer foundation.

He leaned against the car and waited for the officers to come get him.

"Officer! Arrest that little punk! He assaulted me!" Steve screamed as a couple of policemen neared.

188

One officer looked at the other. "I didn't see anything. Did you?"

"No. I think maybe he ran into a door on his way out."

"Look, you fucking assholes, I pay my taxes. I pay your salary, Goddamn it! Now go do your job." Steve demanded.

One of the officers looked at Jason and back at his stepfather. "Sir, I suggest you settle down before we bring you back inside for resisting arrest. Maybe in doing so you caught an elbow and got a bloody nose."

"A bloody nose? I think it's fucking broken!"

"It very well may be. You should quit struggling." The cop said. The second one approached Jason. In fact, he was a young guy not much older than Jason.

"Look, Jacob, is it? Jason? OK, Jason. You can't help judging people in this job. When I was in Afghanistan, a little old lady carrying what we thought was a baby was actually a suicide bomber and killed two of my friends. You're only allowed a few seconds to assess the situation, sometimes you have to choose real quick, and hope you chose wisely. I only told you that so you can get an idea of how tough this job is. It would be easy to believe your dad and say 'Lock him up' and be done with this."

"Stepfather." Jason corrected him.

"Stepfather. Here's the thing. You get tossed in here for possession, and you say 'please. Thank you.' You don't curse us out for doing our job, you call us sir. There is no intent, or even enough here to care about, but you were in the wrong place at the wrong time. Maybe even with the wrong people. I suggest you evaluate them and decide how much you benefit from being their friend. Anyway, your 'fat little prick' of a stepfather is an asshole, but that's his problem. Here's what I'm going to do: lose the paperwork for the weed. No sense having that follow you around while you try to get your shit together. Pay your friends back the bail money. Do you have a safe place to stay?"

"My grandparents."

"You may not believe it, but you're luckier than most. Go home. Your grades decent?" Jason nodded yes. "Good. Stay in school. Decide who your real friends are. Stay at your grandparents, only see your mom if he's not around. He'll make trouble for you if he can, that much I can tell. Get a job, if possible. Helps keep away the boredom that sometimes cause kids to get in trouble. Being a good cop means developing good instincts. My instincts tell me you're not a bad guy. If I see you here again, it means my instincts were wrong, and I don't like to be wrong. Do you understand what I'm saying, Jason?"

"Yes sir."

"Why don't you take off, Jason. Get out of here before you stepdad figures out what's going down. You're a good kid. Don't let that asshole ruin you. I'd like you to succeed so I can rub dear old dad's face in it. Do what you have to do, but don't flush your future down the crapper before you give yourself a chance."

"Thank you, sir. I swear if you ever see me here again it'll to bail out one of my friends." The officer looked at Jason. "You'll never see me again because I won't hang around people who need to be bailed out."

"Good answer, Jason. Here's my card. Hang on to it. You're a good kid. I have faith in you."

Jason watched the cop walk back to his partner and his screaming stepdad. He reached for his wallet to put the officer's card in it. He glanced at the name and it was Billy Flynn, Jr.

Jason got in the car and said, "be cool. He's letting me walk so don't piss him off."

***

Jason followed the policeman's advice. He stayed at his grandparents. His Gramps had a newer model riding lawnmower. If Jason got it running, as long as he did his grandparents' lawn he could use it to make money. Mary Margaret was one of his first clients. She hired him and said it was 'his job to lose.' He thought her odd, but she paid in cash and gave him a tip each month, so she was okay in his book.

Due to his grandparents advanced age, Jason did all the chores. The beginning of his senior year his Gramps died from a heart attack. His Grams needed assisted living and had to sell the house. He was back in his mother's basement for the second half of his senior year, but there was a brightness at the end of the tunnel. Mary Margaret let him store his lawnmower in her garage after his grandparent's house sold. The money went to a nursing home. *At least Steven was robbed of his wife's inheritance,* Jason thought.

He graduated with honors, his mom and his half-siblings there to cheer him on. After he broke his stepdad's nose, Steve barely said two words to Jason.

Mary Margaret took a chance on him. He confessed he couldn't give her a reference or referral. He said, "the only lawn he mowed was his grandparents."

Mary Margaret told him to drive by and show her the lawn. He did, and she hired him. After a while she paid him to do the chores she found unpleasant like grocery shopping or pick up art supplies. Mary Margaret took him to the Warehouse. The idea of having a dedicated creative space blew him away. She saw the look in his eye and made a deal. She'd comp him space for labor. Over time a strong bond grew between the two and the GODZILLA STUDIOS came into existence.

Jason was at a critical point in is life. He wasn't a kid anymore. He couch surfed a place to sleep; when he had no other place to go he slept in the Warehouse. Mary Margaret didn't mind. She knew and if she had a problem with it she would have told him. She allowed him to use the shower at her house and wash his laundry. He needed to make a move. When Brett asked him if he wanted to move to Colorado, all signs pointed to yes, so Jason decided to go. As much as Mary Margaret wanted him to stay; she gave him her full support.

She gave him an envelope and told him to open it exactly at the mid point between there and Denver. He did as he was told. Inside were two smaller envelopes. He opened the first envelope, it was from Mary Margaret. She kept it brief to minimize the tears on each end, but she wanted to give him a little something to get him started. It contained a prepaid Visa for $250. The second card was from John with the name of his contact in Denver. It also contained a prepaid Visa for $250. Jason fought back the tears.

Brett took one look at it and said, "Dude. They're each for $2500. That's five grand."

Jason looked at the one from John. Jason was beyond tears. Two people he wasn't even related to cared that much about him to give him the most money he's ever had in his whole life. He thought he finally understood what it meant to have a family. It was being a part of something bigger than yourself. It was people who had your back. It was people who thought enough of you that you were worth the investment. He sent Mary Margaret a photo of the cards with THANK YOU & JOHN. MISSING YOU GUYS ALREADY. They gassed up, got back on the highway, and headed west.

Chapter Thirteen

Casey was more than happy to host Thanksgiving. Her father's family was coming, Seth too. Jason would leave an empty seat at the table, but John decided to stay, so he sat there. His excuse was to be in town to help Emmy, but Emmy was a pro and didn't need John's help. He subbed in for Jason at the Warehouse, allowing Mary Margaret to bang out canvases. She finished several big canvases, and the drying rack aided the process. Mary Margaret was quieter than usual. She didn't talk when she worked. Mary Margaret walked in circles around the canvas, adding and moving paint around until satisfied. John couldn't figure out how she knew when a piece was done.

"It's hard, but you get an eye for what type of balance you want, and when you think you're almost there, you stop; otherwise, that last stroke will tip the balance and ruin it. I can't tell you how many I've messed up going one step too far. You're good, John, but you're no Jason." Mary Margaret said and put her pallet knife down.

She walked over to John and unpromptedly put her arms around him. He was shocked at her; this was the first time she had reached out, but he quickly put his arms around her before she changed her mind. He tried to inhale the lavender smell of her hair without being obvious, but she looked so pretty, smelled so good, and felt so right. He wanted this moment to last forever.

"John, I miss Jason. I mean, I *miss* him. What will I do when you leave at the end of the month? I finally get some friends, and they start dropping like flies."

"If you want me to, I can stay through the end of the year. Since it's remote, I can do what I need from anywhere."

"I would, but it would be solely for selfish reasons."

"Selfish reasons? Not because you won't be able to go on without me?"

"That's a story for another day. Unfortunately, I'm good at going alone. I'd like you to help me clear this place out. I'm going to leave here by the end of the year."

"How long have you been thinking about that?" John asked, surprised.

"Awhile. After all that trouble last summer, they took away my stripes. I initially thought about it because I was mad. I was being petty, I guess. Like 'so there! I'm taking my crayons and going home!' I never did anything about it. Now Jason's gone. I'll tell you a secret. I knew a bit about Jason's home life and how erratic it was, and one of the reasons I kept this place was that he always had somewhere to go. He had his key. He could come here and escape his stress and use his artistic skills to express whatever was bothering him." She took a step back and looked at John.

"My objective was to see if the arts could make a difference with kids who started life with the cards stacked against them. He proved my point. It can. I knew what a dick his stepdad was, and if he didn't have this, what would have happened to him? His mother wasn't going to step up. He would have been lost to the streets. He would have stopped trying. But he didn't. Jason hung in there, and he came here when things got too much. Look where he is now, on his way to a great future. So, my experiment worked. I saved one kid. You can't save them all, but I saved one. Let somebody else be the hero. There are fifteen studios, and if each saved one kid, that's fifteen kids on their way to a better life. Well, fourteen. I already saved mine.

"But it doesn't feel the same now. Maybe I lost my optimism, but there's no point in being here. I can go back to doing this," she waved her hand over the canvas, "in my garage. That's where I did it before. Maybe even scale back a bit."

"Mary Margaret, I'm surprised to hear all of this. I thought you loved this place."

"I did, but things changed. Not just one thing, but a lot of little things. It doesn't feel the same anymore. Even when Jason was here, things felt off. I have enough for the two shows I've committed to this spring. It's time now. Like I said, let someone else be the hero. I think we're finished. Let's go get something to eat."

They went to the to-go window because Stella was in the car. Mary Margaret talked about upcoming plans for Thanksgiving. Casey was doing half, John the other half. They needed to negotiate who would use what burners and when. Luckily, Mary Margaret had a double oven. Ben and Sheila, with their boys Brendan and Hayes, and younger sister Perry were coming. They were responsible for the desserts.

Mary Margaret got out great Gramma Welch's fine china and the good silverware. She spent the day polishing that stuff. She couldn't figure why she had it. Since it was Ben's grandmother, it should be at his house. He could give it to Casey as a wedding gift. She got the whole set out, including the serving pieces. All the fine China serving dishes. The embroidered line napkins. She set the table as she went. When she finished, she turned on the crystal chandelier. Wow. *It sure looked pretty. Let the next homeowners with bad taste come along and rip it out;* Mary Margaret thought, *I love that chandelier.* Casey came in and hugged her mother.

"That looks beautiful."

"I'm sure your father won't think so. He'll end up with dishpan hands."

"What's that?"

"What's what? Dishpan hands?"

"Yeah. Those."

"Oh, Casey, I hope you never find out." Mary Margaret said.

***

Thanksgiving morning found Casey and John in the kitchen, working their way through Thanksgiving dinner. Mary Margaret got the appetizers ready and on the table. Ben and his crew came, followed by Seth. The party started with mimosas. Seth offered to be the bartender. He made them, and Ben served them. They invited Casey and John in from the kitchen for a toast.

"Let's give a toast. Here's to our family and friends, for which we give thanks," said Ben, not the most eloquent of speakers. Everyone echoed 'here, here" and sipped from their fanciest champagne flutes.

"Ow." Said Casey. "There's something wrong with the ice."

"Here. Let me see," said Seth and stuck his finger in her glass. "This must be it." He dropped down on one knee. "Casey Miller Welch, will you marry me?" The room went silent. All eyes looked at Casey. She burst into tears. "Yes, Seth Howard Green, yes, I will marry you." The room broke out in applause. The women went into the kitchen to wash off the ring and admire it. The men went to the couch to watch football.

"You didn't know?" Sheila asked Mary Margaret. "He asked Ben for her hand in marriage, and they created this whole set up."

"I did not. I am shocked. Speechless. Casey had no idea. Seth was lucky she didn't swallow it. It's good she got the ring before she knew her dad was involved. If she knew he asked her father that archaic tradition, she might've thrown the ring in his face. Nobody makes decisions like that for Casey."

"That's true. She's like her mom that way. So, Seth is sentimental, a romantic. A traditionalist. He said he wanted to do it the 'right way.'"

Casey came over to her mom and stepmother. "Oh. Wow. Can you believe this?" She said and stuck out her hand so they could admire the ring.

Mary Margaret hugged her daughter. "Oh, sweetie, congratulations. He looks like one of the good ones."

"He is, Mom, he is."

"John is getting tense. He wants to get back on his turf before Casey steals a burner." Mary Margaret shooed them out of the kitchen. She sat at the table while everybody else joined in the family room. John looked out and saw her sitting alone. He left his precious burner and came over to sit next to her.

"Mary Margaret," John said. "Wow. That's some news."

"I know. Casey was so surprised. Me, too."

"Are you okay?"

"Yes. Seth is a great guy. She's a great girl. They'll get married and have a great life."

John made a face at her.

"I mean it. I do. A while ago, we talked. Casey asked me how I would feel if, after she was done with school, she went out to see the world. I told her that's what she was supposed to do, and that's what I expected her to do. But get married? That, I did not see coming. It's fine, though. I just need a minute."

"I have to get back there, or Casey will sabotage my dishes," John said.

"Put too much salt in your sweet potatoes?"

"Heaven forbid!" He rushed back into the kitchen.

Since there were only nine of them, they all ate at the main table. It was crowded with food and people, like being a judge at the state fair. Mary Margaret took her plate, passed it and said: "Just put a spoonful of everything on it and keep it going until it comes back." It was a good idea. It would be crazy if they passed each dish around as well as fill their plates.

The wine flowed, shouts and laughter punctuated the conversation. Even Ben's kids joined in, not quite yet the dispassionate, too cool for family teenagers they would morph into as they aged.

"So you had no idea he was going to propose?" Sheila asked Casey.

"No. None."

"Seth. What if she said no?" John kidded.

"It was the only way I could get her to move to Atlanta. Casey said she wasn't going to waste her time following around a promise. She said to put a ring on it, so I did."

"Atlanta?" Mary Margaret asked.

Casey's face suddenly turned white. "Oh, Mom. Seth has a six-month fellowship. It starts January 1st. I want to go with him."

"When do you leave?"

"In a month. After Christmas." Casey said with an Uh-Oh tone in her voice.

Her mom smiled at her. "Casey. What did I tell you? You were only on loan from God. I knew the day they placed you in my arms I knew some guy was going to come along and make you a better offer. I'm just glad it's Seth. He's a good guy, and he's crazy about you. I didn't realize how close you were, although you did tell me he might be the one. I wish you nothing but joy. Besides, I can come to visit and stay as long as I want."

"That's right, Mom. Any time and you can stay as long as you want."

"You better ask Seth how he feels about it before you make an offer like that. What about school?"

"I've got enough clinical hours; now it's just bookwork. I can do that remote."

"Here you go, Casey. Tomorrow is the first day of the rest of your life. Lives," and raised a glass to her. "Well done, my darlin'. I'm very proud of you."

John noticed again Mary Margaret seemed quieter than usual. She smiled at the right times and laughed at the right moments, but she had the same look in her eye as she did when reflecting upon Jason. He wasn't sure if he saw cracks in her facade or if it was the lighting, but John sensed her shift but not in a good way.

John stayed until everyone left to talk to her, but she told him to go. Mary Margaret was tired, she said, and just wanted to go to bed. She shooed him out and watched him leave. *Everyone leaves sooner or later,* she thought, turned out the lights, and headed off to bed.

***

Mary Margaret gave her notice to Malik that she wasn't going to be needing the studio space anymore. Malik invited her for a cup of coffee in the cafe. Mary

Margaret wanted to tell him she was done and not discuss it any further, but Malik was a friend, so she agreed to talk to him.

"What is it?" He asked her. "The real reason. Was it because of what happened last summer?"

"To be honest, yes. Not about here, but about me. It's funny, or maybe sad, but the girls started treating me like a hero or something 'cuz I set that kid on fire.' I was developing a reputation for the wrong reasons.

"I had to figure out why I lit that torch. It was because the boy had the girl by the neck. That set something off internally. I swear to God, if he didn't let her go, I might have done something. That's not what the whole program was about; it was about peace and love, and happiness. No negativity. I even wrote that in the mission statement. I violated my own policy.

"The other reason is Jason left. He moved to Colorado. That's great for him, but not so good for me. I never realized how much I depended on him. He was practically an unpaid assistant or intern. I don't know how I'm going to manage. I just want some time to figure out what's next. I'm not a part of this place anymore. I'm simply a tenant. As a tenant, keeping this place is not a wise business decision. I can go back to doing it in my garage. But with Jason gone, this whole place makes me sad. I need a break from it all. I have help to clean it out the first couple of weeks of December, so I'll be out by the end of the month."

"Mary Margaret, there's nothing I can say or do to get you to stay? You were such a big part of this place."

"'You were.' That's me in the past tense. So no, I can't stay. That was part of my punishment. My participation is not allowed. It was a great experience, and I hope you get support from everyone else to keep it going. I think the neighborhood benefited from it. It helped kids to cope with the boredom of a rootless summer, but I don't think I have it in me to continue. You are a great guy and a wonderful person, but you can't talk me into staying." Mary Margaret said, her tone was such that he knew trying to change her mind was a waste of his breath.

John helped Mary Margaret clean her studio out. It took up only a couple of afternoons; most of her things were big and bulky but not heavy. Having a truck made sense. After the last load, she had to lock up and leave the keys for Malik. For the last time, Mary Margaret shut and locked the door. She felt sad she'd never go into that room again. Ever. She held the keys in her hand and looked at the closed door.

Jason made a poster that said 'Godzilla Studio. Enter at your own risk.' He painted a cartoon Godzilla rising from the ocean and taped it up on the door. The last thing she did was carefully remove the sign. Once it was off, the closed door looked like all the others. With an ache in her chest, Mary Margaret gently rolled up the sign. The Godzilla Studio was no more. She dropped the keys into the suggestion box by the freight elevator when she and John left the building for the last time. He hugged her before they got in her truck. He leaned against the side of her vehicle and held her while she cried silent tears. When she finished mourning what was or what used to be, she pulled away from John and wiped her face with the back of her hand. "Let's go," was all she said.

They left the lot and headed towards home. He rolled up to the Stop sign on the corner when Mary Margaret noticed a group of kids standing around. She waved to them. A couple waved back.

Chapter Fourteen

It was good breaking down her studio didn't take too long; John was prepping for his contract in Tulsa and pretty busy with conference calls. He had at least one a day. They stored her studio in her garage. It was a two-car garage and had plenty of room if Mary Margaret wanted to set it back up, but for right now, she wanted it in storage. John was concerned about Mary Margaret; her personality seemed dimmed somehow. He couldn't say precisely what was wrong other than she was quieter than usual.

John ran into her at the grocery store. He was in the bread aisle, and Mary Margaret was over by the canned goods. He pushed his cart over to say hi when he saw a strange man approach her. John stopped and watched as the man said something to her. He reached out and grabbed her forearm in a firm grasp. It looked like Mary Margaret wanted to leave, and the man was preventing her from doing so. John approached to help her. They were in a heated discussion and didn't notice John as he neared.

"Let go of me! Let go of me, or I'll scream!" Mary Margaret said as she tried to pull her arm from his grasp, but he wouldn't let go.

"Mary Margaret? Do you need help?" John asked her. They both turned to face him. Mary Margaret was as white as butcher's paper; the blood vanished from her face her eyes huge with desperation.

"Hey, Mary Margaret! This your new boyfriend? Does she still like to take it up the ass?" He said to John and let go of her arm with a cruel laugh.

Once her arm was free, Mary Margaret bolted from the store, leaving her cart and groceries blocking the aisle. She ran for the door and was gone.

John froze in place. He saw her run, he looked at the guy, and John ran over in his mind what had just happened.

The man spoke to John. "She's a real wildcat in the sack, ain't she? She's down for anything, and I mean anything."

John's first instinct was to run after Mary Margaret, confused by what the guy said. After the man spoke again, John followed his second instinct and hauled off and punched the guy right in the mouth. He wasn't expecting it and kissed the floor. He was right in front of an endcap display of canned tomatoes. John stepped over the guy to find Mary Margaret but first knocked a couple of cans out from the bottom, and the whole display rained down on Dan Bauer as he lay on the floor holding his split lip.

John left his cart and groceries next to the pile of tomato cans and the guy yelling from underneath them. He ran to the parking lot, but Mary Margaret was long gone. John drove to her house and saw no sign of her. He knew the code to open the garage door. Once the door was up, he saw her car and tried the kitchen door, but it was locked from inside. John had an important conference call he needed to take and called Ben. He briefly described the scene at the store, but he had no answer about what happened.

Ben had the key to get inside the house and would come right over so John could make his call. John wanted to wait until Ben came, but he couldn't. He had to leave.

John left, and Ben soon arrived. He opened the door, but the house was quiet.

"Mary Margaret? You here?" Ben called out but was met with silence. He walked towards the bedrooms. "Mary Margaret? You here? We're starting to worry." Stella whined, she was on the wrong side of the door, but nothing but silence answered them. Ben tried the bedroom door, but it was locked. "I know you're in there. Are you okay?"

"Yes. Now go."

"I don't think I should leave. John was quite concerned."

The thought of John bearing witness to the things Dan Bauer said about her was cemented was mind and played over and over in a continuous loop. She started to cry and then she started to sob. Loud, endless sobs that wouldn't stop.

202

"Marym? Please open the door. You're starting to scare me." She didn't answer and continued crying.

"You're really scaring me now. I'm going to call Sheila." More sobs but still no answer. Ben called Sheila and asked her to leave work. "Please come as soon as you can. John wasn't sure what happened, but I think she's having a breakdown. Maybe she'll talk to you. Hurry. Please."

Sheila left work and met Ben in the kitchen.

"Ben, what's going on? What's got her so upset?"

"I'm not sure. John called me. He saw Mary Margaret at the store, she was arguing with some guy. He had a hold of her arm, gripped really hard and she couldn't get free. John went over to help, and the guy said some horrible things about Mary Margaret. She freaked out and took off."

Ben rubbed his forehead. "I guess the guy said some things to John and John slugged him one and a big display of canned food fell on the guy. He couldn't find Mary Margaret in the parking lot so he came here but couldn't get inside. John called and asked me to come, he had to take off for a while, but I think he's coming back. Anyway, she's locked herself in her room and she's crying, Sheila, she's crying like somebody died. Maybe she'll talk to you."

"Sure. I wonder who it was."

"John said he'd never seen him before."

"Let me try to talk to her," Sheila walked over to the door and tried the handle. It was still locked; she was still crying on the other side of the door.

"Mary Margaret? It's me, Sheila. Can I come in? We're getting worried about you." Mary Margaret didn't answer. "Please? Just me? Maybe I can help." No answer except more sobbing.

"Ben. Give me a credit card. I'll pop the lock."

He got out his wallet and gave her a card. "You know how to do that?"

"Please. Parent of teenagers." She took the card, jimmied it a few times, and the lock gave way. She handed him back his card and opened the door a crack.

"Mary Margaret? It's me. It's just me coming in." She went in and shut the door. Mary Margaret was curled into the fetal position on her bed, her face to the wall, crying. Sheila grabbed some tissues and sat on the bed. She reached out and touched Mary Margaret's shoulder. The way she crumpled herself in a ball scared Sheila; it looked almost looked like she was boneless. "Please, honey, whatever it is, it can't be that bad."

Mary Margaret rolled to face Sheila. Sheila handed her some tissues. She wiped her eyes and blew her nose. "It *can* be that bad. It is *that* bad. I'll tell you, but I'm never going to talk about it again. Ever." She laid on her back and looked at the ceiling. "Remember that guy your cousin Billy Flynn helped me with? It was him. When I first met him, it was the most incredible rush I ever experienced. I mean, he was all over me and I never had a free moment to myself. He was consumed with me. How stupid was I? It was a huge red flag I completely ignored."

"I liked the attention. I thought it was that mad passion Ben always said our marriage lacked. I thought, 'here it is' and let myself get sucked into it. After a bit I realized it was too much and tried to slow it down. Instead, he came at me full force. It got to the point I wasn't allowed to say no. There was no point in saying no. If I did, he hounded me until I said yes. Things in the bedroom. If I didn't want to have sex, he hammered at me until I consented. I did it so he would stop yelling at me. Other things he wanted if I didn't want it, he just steamrolled over me anyway. I said no, and he did it anyway. I remembered crying afterwards and he said I was ruined, and no other guy would want me if they knew how dirty I was, and he laughed at me. He laughed."

"That's why I got Billy Flynn involved. I had to get away from him. He fucked up my head big time. I was convinced he was right. I know the logic of it all, I saw a therapist for a long time, but I couldn't ever get beyond the emotion of it. I was no good. He was right. No normal guy would want me. I was so ashamed. I still am." She paused to wipe her nose. "It was only when Ben said Casey was being ignored a lightbulb went off."

"He wanted me to send Casey to live with you guys because he wanted to move in; I finally realized I had to get out. That's when Billy Flynn got involved. When it was over, I talked to a counselor, but I could never forgive myself. I felt like I was two people. The one before, who everyone knew and liked, and the one after. I wasn't the same person. I was weak and damaged. I was ashamed and *scared.*"

"I was so afraid and ashamed I let that happen. I thought everyone I loved would turn away from me if they knew the truth. I don't know if it was a tattoo or a scar, but it permanently marked me as less than. I still believe all that shit he said about me, about no guy would want me if they knew the truth. That's why I never dated. I was so afraid of the rejection of liking someone who would find out how dirty I was they'd walk away."

"For years, I was so afraid of exactly what happened today. Of running into him and having him expose my every sin. It happened. In front of John. My worst nightmare happened, and John's probably halfway to Tulsa." Mary Margaret finished, her voice caught in her throat, and she started sobbing. She rolled away and curled into herself.

"Hey," Sheila said quietly, "you know, don't you, you were the victim of a brutal sexual assault? I'm not sure, but I think numerous violent sexual assaults. Not assaults. Rape, Mary Margaret. You were raped."

"No." Mary Margaret said with an edge to her voice, "I should have been stronger. I allowed it to happen. It's on me. It's my fault."

"You're wrong. You did say no. He didn't care. He exploited you. He *used* you. That asshole twisted you in knots until he had you right where he wanted. You couldn't say no because you were afraid of what would happen. You had no chance. You have a beautiful, loving heart willing to give anyone the benefit of doubt, and he used it against you. The only thing you're guilty of is wanting to be loved."

Mary Margaret cried and kept crying. She couldn't stop. Sheila stayed and rubbed her back and kept telling her she was okay, but Mary Margaret cried on, repeating over and over, "I should have stopped it. I should have been stronger. I should have never talked to John. It's never going to be okay. Never." Shelia was at a loss what to do, she was unable to reach Mary Margaret. She curled herself into a ball and cried on.

"Honey, I'm going to leave for a minute. I'll be right back."

She left the room but left the door open a hair in case Mary Margaret called for her, but Mary Margaret seemed to be lost in the pain of her past. She couldn't stop crying because she felt so ashamed. Ashamed and embarrassed. Mary Margaret thought by now everyone at the grocery store heard and by now she was the talk of the town. Her ugly secret laid bare for all to see and judge her, her shame on display in aisle nine.

"Ben, I'm getting kind of worried. She seems locked in her head, and I can't reach her."

"What was it? I can't imagine what set her off."

"Who. Not What. Who. Remember Dan Bauer? That guy she dated for a while and Billy had to get involved? Him. Ben, he abused her. Emotionally, physically, and sexually. She told me some really scary shit. She has it ingrained in her brain it's all her fault. That's what he did. He manipulated her, convinced her, every time she said no it didn't matter. He did it anyway. She said it didn't matter, he's right. She's dirty; no self-respecting man would want anything to do with her.

"That's why she hasn't dated in over fifteen years. Like if a good guy liked her, he wouldn't after he knew the 'real' her. Ben, she saw a therapist to work through it and still thinks it was all her fault. 'I should have been stronger,' she keeps repeating."

"Really? She hid it so well. Even when we were in court, she never mentioned it, and she should have. I knew that guy was an asshole, but she seemed so into him I didn't say anything to her."

"I guess, for lack of a better phrase, he love bombed her. She was lonely, and he took advantage of that. He romanced the hell out of her, and she said it felt good. She was a sucker and fell for every phony bouquet of roses or candlelight dinner. Once he had her hooked, the abuse started. He would blame it on her; if he was rude or mean to her, it was her fault. It was always her fault if he wasn't happy.

"I think she thought if she could make him happy it would get better. If she tried harder, it would get better. If she gave in it would get better, or at least stop. I think you're the one that woke her up. He wanted to cut Casey out of her life so she could devote herself totally to him. He wanted to send Casey to move in with us. You told her Casey said her mom ignored her all the time because he was always calling and not spending time with her. When it came to it was either him or Casey, she chose Casey, and that's when you and Billy stepped in. She suffered some significant trauma. I'm not surprised by the pain she's experiencing.

"She said it was her worst fear somebody would find out and judge her, and that's what happened today. It happened in front of John. She's never said so, but I think she kind of liked John, and I think he likes her. She's convinced now that he knows the 'real her' he's going to judge her, find her less than, and never want to see her again. That's what she told me, mostly, and I filled in some of the details. But Ben, she's stuck on the fact that she was weak. In her mind she's responsible because she wasn't stronger."

"Well, John was the one who called me. He ran after her, but she was gone. He found her car, but the door to the house was locked. John said Mary Margaret was in trouble and needed help, so I came. I had a key and went inside but she locked herself in her room. I tried to talk to her, but she wouldn't open the door, so I called you."

"What did he say to John?"

"He didn't say, but he said enough that John decked him and left him on the floor."

"Wow."

"Before he left, he knocked down a display of canned tomatoes that landed all over him."

"John doesn't strike me as that type."

"I guess if you push a man far enough, he'll do anything." Ben's phone rang. "It's John. Hi. Yeah, Sheila came. Sure, why don't you. We'll be here. Goodbye." Ben turned to Sheila. "John's coming over, and hopefully we can sort this out.

Do you think we should tell him what Marym told you? I mean, it is her business. It's her story to tell, not ours."

"Depends on what John knows. If he knows only that guy's version, it's only fair he knows hers."

"Yes. I think she's afraid he's going to judge her. He's gonna say 'boy, I'm sure glad I never got involved with you,' and be on the first flight out of here." Sheila said.

"No. He's frantic with worry. He packed a bag and plans on staying here until she's okay. He has an eight-a.m. meeting in Tulsa on January third. He's staying and not leaving until the second."

"How come? I wonder." Sheila said.

"You suck as a girl. He's in love with her." Ben shook his head.

"No! When did he tell you that?"

"He didn't. I don't think he knows. You wait. He'll come walking in here and make a beeline for you; worried about Mary Margaret. He'll fret."

"Fret?"

"Fret. Just you watch." Ben said confidently.

That's what happened, John came in went straight to Sheila. He wanted to see Mary Margaret, but Sheila advised against it. She wanted them to compare notes. John went first.

"I was at the store, and I saw Mary Margaret. I thought I'd say hello when suddenly this guy grabbed her by the arm. I thought she was in trouble and went over to help. I'm not sure I should say this next part, but what he said was 'hey you're her boyfriend, he said some rude and downright vulgar things, and she took off. The guy said a few other disgusting things, so I punched him. All these cans fell down, but I didn't stick around. What do you know?" Ben and Sheila looked at each other. "Come on, you guys."

"Well, you know you said some things were hard to say, some might be even harder to hear. Sheila can tell you what she they talked about."

Sheila started in on Mary Margaret's story. John listened without interruption. At the end he took his index fingers and wiped the corners of his eyes.

"Poor Mary Margaret. All these years, and nobody knew. She's hurting from so many other things right now, no wonder it feels like the bottom dropped out of her life."

"What other things?"

"She didn't tell you? She's finished at the Warehouse. At the summer camp she tried to break up this fight, it wasn't really a fight, this guy was choking a girl. She told him to stop. He said make me, and she lit her blowtorch and told him she'd light him up like a Christmas tree."

"Oh, dear," said Sheila. Ben laughed under his breath. "Stop it Ben. It's not funny. Well, it is, but just stop."

"Wait. There's more. Because of her actions, she's off the board and any committees. She's just a tenant now. Plus, Jason left. He moved to Denver. It felt too lonely there without him, so she gave up the studio. She doesn't want the space anymore. And Casey's news. She's overjoyed for her, but it does make her terribly sad. Casey won't be popping by with coffee anymore, and I'm leaving.

"It will just be the three of you, and you'll be busy with the kids. I guess it all piled up and that dick today came right out of left field. I think she felt all these losses at once, and today she remembered she's always going to be alone. She's convinced herself she deserves to be alone." He reached into his pocket and gave Sheila a bottle. Anti-anxiety, in case she can't sleep, or can't stop crying."

"Aren't you staying overnight?" Ben asked.

"I am, but maybe she might not be open to me being here. Tell her I'm here for security or if she needs something, but she doesn't have to talk to me. I'm only here to make sure she has everything she needs."

Sheila went in to talk to Mary Margaret. She told her John was staying and he would be on the couch.

"He's only here in case of an emergency, you don't have to talk to him. John talked to Dan at the store and knocked him out. He talked to me, got your side of the story, and understands completely what happened to you," Sheila assured her.

"John said it didn't matter to him, but it mattered to you, so he is respectfully backing away. He doesn't want to put any more stress on you. John said he could love you if only you would let him. Actually," Sheila said, "I that last part up I made up, but I believe he would."

Mary Margaret nodded in acknowledgment but said nothing and kept her eyes closed. She didn't take a pill; Sheila left the bottle and a glass of water on her nightstand for later. She made sure Mary Margaret was all set for the night. John was there so she wasn't alone. They would check on her tomorrow. She and Ben were leaving unless she needed anything else. Mary Margaret stayed curled in her ball and said nothing.

John sat in her family room, powered up his computer, and got ahead of the work he had to get finished before they advanced to the next step. He kept an ear out for Mary Margaret but only heard silence from her room. It was only after he got a good chunk of his work finished, he allowed himself to let his mind wander about what happened to Mary Margaret, both in the past and today.

Judging by that guy in the grocery store, it explained why she wasn't interested in any romantic entanglements. Maybe she had poor judgement in men. Or maybe bad luck. That guy damaged her. It colored how she viewed herself over the past fifteen years. She rewrote the script from that prick being violent and predatory as the cause of her trauma, to its being her fault because she was weak and should have stopped it. John thought if he knew the whole story yesterday, it would have been more than canned tomatoes that rained down on that asshole.

John turned this over in his head while he brushed his teeth and got ready for bed. He stopped by Mary Margaret's door and listened. All was quiet so he returned to the couch to watch a little TV before he went to sleep. He awoke in the night to the blue light of the TV; he turned it off and went back to sleep. John woke again to Mary Margaret gently shaking him. He rolled over to look at her.

"Mary Margaret, are you okay? What do you need?" he softly asked her.

"You know how you like to hold my hand? Would you come hold it now?" Her voice trembled. "I don't feel so good. Like what's left of me is a big hole I can't cross."

"Sure. There's not a lot of room here, but I'll squish over."

"Let's go in my room. It'll be more comfortable."

"I just have on a tee shirt and boxers. Let me put on some sweats."

"That's OK. I feel like I'm done crying, but I don't know what's coming next. I'm scared."

He stood up and took her hand. "Come on. Things always seem worse at night. We can talk in the morning if you want." They went into her room and got in bed. "Now get comfortable, I'll fill in around you. She turned on her side.

"Here. Roll over." She asked. He did. "Give me your hand." Mary Margaret took his arm and pulled it over her waist. She took his hand and held it up against her chest. "This OK for you?"

"Yes, it's perfect. Go to sleep. You're safe, I won't let anyone hurt you. Goodnight, Mary Margaret."

"Goodnight, John. Thank you."

"Shh. Go to sleep."

He didn't want to think about the last time he slept with a woman, when he actually slept with one. He was the king of early morning meetings. As in 'I'd love to stay but..' as an exit strategy. Even on weekends. He did business internationally, or so he said. What's a Sunday morning here could be Monday afternoon in Australia or Japan.

Laying next to Mary Margaret, her body warm and soft, he felt a sense of contentment he hadn't felt in ages, if ever. As a young man it wasn't sleep he was after, as he aged, a good night's sleep became his priority. He figured if you looked around it was pretty easy to find someone interested in day time

211

lovemaking; avoiding the stay-the-night conversation. John would take her out for a nice dinner, walk her to the door, and say he'd call. He always did call; even if he wasn't going to be around for a second date, it was courtesy. John figured it was what a woman who gave him an evening of her time deserved. He drifted off to sleep, comforted by the warmth of Mary Margaret's body.

***

The sun was up. John looked at his watch. Seven a.m. He needed to take a leak. Hopefully, she remembered she invited him in last night. *That's all Mary Margaret needed, waking up next to someone she didn't expect. That would surely send her over the edge,* he thought. He removed his hand from hers and rolled away. He got up and used the hallway bathroom.

John went back to look in on her; she was still in the same position with her eyes closed. During the night Stella jumped up on the bed and Mary Margaret curled around her. Stella looked at John, daring him to make her move. "You're fine, Stella. Come find me if you want to go out."

John put on his sweats and made a pot of coffee; grabbed his computer to get started on that day's business. He was going through his email when he looked up and saw her standing in the doorway watching him. She had on her thick, white Turkish terry cloth bath robe, a wicked case of bed head, and a serious look on her face.

"Hey, good morning. Can I get you a cup of coffee?" He returned her serious look with one of his own.

"No, I can get it. Keep working," Mary Margaret said and opened the sliding door to let Stella out. She fixed a cup of coffee, sat down and watched him work. After a bit he looked up. John remained silent and gave her room to speak. She didn't say anything. They looked at each other. John thought she might be embarrassed by the whole thing yesterday, so he would give her a break and speak first.

"Surprised to see me?" He asked.

"No."

212

"Glad to see me?"

"Yes. Kinda. Sorta."

"Mind explaining that? I'm not sure what you mean."

"I feel grateful. Glad. Lucky. I also feel stupid and embarrassed. Ashamed. Mortified. Naked and Afraid." She said.

"Like the TV show?"

"Just the good parts."

"Those are the good parts." He sipped his mug. "Look, I'm going to tell you all I know. You can confirm, deny or pass. At least you'll know what might be out there in the ether. You heard him. He said 'hey you are Mary Margaret's new boyfriend? You heard what he said after that. You ran out and he said 'she's a real wildcat in bed.' I punched him in the mouth, dumped a display of canned tomatoes on him, and came here, but the door was locked."

"I called Ben because I had something I had to do for work. He had a key so he could get inside and check on you. When I got back Ben and Sheila were here. Sheila talked to you, and she's come to the opinion that you suffered significant emotional and physical damage during your relationship with that guy in the grocery store. I understand the extent and type of injuries, so you don't have to ever talk about them. I know it all, and none of it matters. For the record, you were the victim of repeated sexual assaults. Every time you said 'NO,' if it went any further, it says a lot about him, and very little about you."

"Yeah, so you say." Mary Margaret looked at him. "I'll let you in on a secret. You're old. I'm old. You don't have time to waste waiting for me to be un-fucked up. I spent years trying to change how I looked at it. To 'reframe it.' To view it as no longer a defining moment in my life. But I never got past it or around it and I'm sure as hell not gonna relive it, so thank you, but been there, done that. I am so grateful to have you here. I'm sorry I can't offer you more."

"I'm not looking for more. Look. I'm working on a plan, but it's not finished. When I have all the parts in place I'll ask you what you think about it. In my opinion, and this is just based off of what I know, I think I can help you. As far as what I want from you, the answer is nothing except for you to heal. So do whatever you need to do. Rest up. I'm going to talk to Mark Stewart to see if he could if recommend a good therapist."

"What? Why? Who says?" She started to fidget in her seat, one of her tells when she got nervous.

"I know you just want to take what happened, put in a box on the top shelf the closet, and stop thinking about it. That's okay for now. That strategy may have worked for years, but you'll never be able to completely move forward if you still allow that prick to take up real estate in your head. He's not worth the brain cells. You need to talk to a grief counselor first."

"A grief counselor? Whatever for? Nobody died."

"No, but metaphorically, yes. You need to remember Jason and smile, not get all weepy. Casey moving away has got be hard to process, it came right out of the blue. With the loss of your studio and your role at the Warehouse, you've got a little of everything hanging around your neck, and you're crushed under the weight of it all. You'll end up afraid to leave the house. Once you've reconciled the past; you can look forward to the future. A future where you make plans for the rest of your life."

"Plans. Future plans? Like what?"

"Leaving this place. Why stay here? All those things you can't 'reframe' or reimagine, why not leave them here? All those horrible memories, fuck 'em. Leave them here. Nobody says you have to drag all that shit around for the rest of your life."

"Where am I supposed to go?"

"Wherever I am."

"Huh? I don't get it."

John looked at her and wondered how much to say. "I can't tell you how being here has shown me how much my life is missing. Usually, I blow into town, do the job and leave. I do that on purpose, specifically to avoid getting too involved with any eligible females. I was a bachelor and happy about it. However, I love being here. I love *you*.

"I forgot what it was like to have place at the table. Ben, Sheila, Casey, Jason, even Stella; there's a sense of family here. I had a family once. I'd like to be closer to my boys. I'd like to be closer to you. I love you. The time we spend together is wonderful, even the bad parts. Let's take the past and bury it. Come with me. Let's do something fun, unencumbered by the past. Let's look forward to the future."

"What are you saying?" *Did he just tell me he loves me?* She thought.

"I'm saying I'm staying until I leave for Tulsa. I don't want you left alone. I care about you. Like I said, I love you. When you feel ready, you come join me, if that's what you want to do. Mary Margaret, I refuse to let you punish yourself any further, whatever the outcome. If moving forward means you leave me in the past as well, so be it. You're at a crossroads in your life.

"You can't change what happened, but you can consider it a chapter in your life that's been over for a long time. You can forgive yourself. Let go of the shame. The blame. The responsibility of it all. It happened. It's out there. It's *over*. Don't let it ruin the rest of your life. Forgive yourself and let something good fill the space releasing it all will create. Let *me* fill that space. I promise I will never hurt you, and I won't let anything else hurt you, either." John said, looking in her eyes to see if anything was getting through. "As long as you love me, nothing else matters."

"Love me? Why? I'm a mess, John. Join you? Why would I join you?"

"Come. Let's sit on the couch. I want to run some things by you." He led her into family room. "I just want to ask you a few things. I like you, and I think you like me too. If we could get away from all this, could you love me?"

"What do you mean?" Her eyes widened. She asked the question to buy some time. She knew what he meant.

"Like you pointed out earlier, we're old. Or older. Or oldish. We don't have time to waste deciding what comes next, so let's decide now. I want to be in love

215

again. I want a partner. I want to know someone is waiting for me at the end of day. Not just anybody. You. I don't care about any of it other than how it hurt you. As long as we're together, I'll do anything for you.

"It probably will be different than any other kind of love we've been in, but that's good. It will be on our own terms. I want to wake up in the middle of the night and snuggle back to sleep next to you. I want to wake up in the morning and bring you coffee. What do you think?"

"I'm not sure, this is kind of sudden. I've never thought about it. I figured being alone was my destiny. I thought it was a life sentence written on my soul, a stain I'd have to live with for the rest of my life."

"Well, think about it. There isn't a stain on your soul. It's an episode of your life that's over. Thank God, you realized it now and don't waste any more time thinking about. Not to minimize what happened, but it's old news. Daylight's burning. Do you want to be in love? With me, I mean."

"You know, I don't think I've ever been in love. All my loves were stacked to fail because they weren't with guys who were available. Like Ben. I love him as much as I ever did, but he was never mine to have. So, are you saying you could love me if I let you?"

"Yes. I already said that. What I want to know is could you love me? As long as you love me, nothing else matters. I promise I will never hurt you."

Mary Margaret sat a minute and thought about what he said to her; about everything. "I think I could. I think it would fun. Yesterday, when you stepped up to the plate for me, I think I finally felt how love is supposed to feel. It's kind of messy, and it means you have to figure out the important order of things. You didn't worry about my behavior or reputation. None of that is important to you, but I am. You were worried about me. You cared about me.

"My big fears of who could ever love or want me blew up. You could love me. You heard the worst of it right from the horse's mouth, and you didn't care. You were worried about me. I mean, you packed up and moved in to help me."

"Some people might think that was pretty presumptuous. They might not like somebody just moving in and setting up camp. And by the way, horse's ass." John clarified. "Horse's *ass.*"

"Yeah, but when someone you love is in a bad way, you do whatever you can to help. It was so nice to have you here. When I woke up and it was dark, I almost lost it until I remembered you were here. You helped me. Having you here seems right. You might be the yin to my yang." She pushed a loose hank of hair behind her ear. "I think I might love you."

"I think I might love you, too. We're both on same page. Does it bother you I'm here?"

"No. It probably should, but it doesn't. It seems very natural to have you here."

"I'll tell you my plans, you let me know your take on it. I insist that you find a therapist and see her twice a week. You have a lot to process. All the changes over the last six months have been big ones, Mary Margaret.

"You need to chew them over with someone and make your peace with it all. Then you both come up with a strategy to help you understand the past, and how to leave it there.

"I think that's why when you saw that guy pin the girl against the fence, you lost it. Maybe you learned the lesson a little late, but you weren't going to let any other girl go through what you went through. You weren't going to let any guy diminish a girl and let her think she deserved it. Not even if you had to set him on fire to prove him wrong."

"I would have, too. In that moment, I would have."

"But you didn't. Maybe this might help you reframe things. You may have been a victim once, but not anymore. Not you, not anyone you know, not even a stranger, will be a victim if you're there. You learned a hard lesson. But you learned it. You don't need it anymore, but if you have to teach it to someone else, pass the matches."

Mary Margaret looked at him. She raked her fingers through her hair.

"After this, you join me, and we take some time bumming around. We can settle here for the summer or sell it all and start out fresh. I think a change of scenery would do you good, but for right now no big decisions need to be made. I'll stay here until I leave for Tulsa. The holidays are coming up soon, we'll celebrate like you usually do. How do you handle the holidays?"

"Ben's for Christmas. Christmas Eve used to be just me and Casey. We'd have a bunch of appetizers and sit by the fire. Very low key. Now she and Seth need to make their own decisions how they want to work the holidays. I wouldn't be surprised if she goes to meet his folks. You solve a lot of problems. Now, no worries about who gets custody of me."

"You surprise me. I expected you to fight me tooth and nail about making changes. The fact that you're open to new ideas has me optimistic."

"I guess there's not a lot of time and I just gotta go with my gut. I lived with that fear, that shame; if anybody knew my deepest and darkest sins, everyone who loved me would turn away. My biggest fear happened, and nothing happened.

"He announced it in the middle of the grocery store, and the ceiling didn't cave in. The world didn't tip off its axis, it's still here. You're still here. So it happened. The funny thing is I'm relieved. I lived with fact it happened, and kept it a secret. I was so scared what would happen if it got out, but it's not a secret anymore. I let can let it go now. It has no power over me.

"My heart says change things up, change things up and do something else. Anything. But you have to talk to Ben and Sheila. This falls into rash and impulsive, and I've never been successful at either. I want them to tell me to go for it. Maybe I hung onto the past because it gave me an excuse not to have much of a future. Now I want one. I want to talk somebody and clean house. Exorcise my demons. Lose that emotional dead weight. Maybe involve you in a session and get ready to be happy."

"I can make you happy. I want to make you happy."

"I think you can, too. This is like Casey's news. Completely out of left field but makes perfect sense." This time, Mary Margaret reached for him, and John took her in his arms. He tightly held on to her.

218

"As long as you love me, Mary Margaret, I'll keep you safe. I'll never let you go."

✳✳✳

Casey's plans for the Holidays did involve going home with Seth and meeting his family. John cooked a feast for the last Sunday before they were due to travel. They invited Ben's crew and had a mini-Christmas to make things easier on Casey and Seth. They had a lot of packing and traveling coming up and time was getting precious. It was during dessert Mary Margaret spoke to Casey.

"Now, Casey, I have something I need to ask. John wants to be my boyfriend. What do you think about that?"

"Do you want to be his girlfriend?"

"Yes, I think I do."

"There you go. Congratulations." Casey sat back and look at her mother. "Wait a minute. For real? You're not kidding?"

"No. I think John and I can be considered an item."

"Did he give you his class ring? Are you going steady?" Casey teased.

"No. We got matching tattoos." Mary Margaret said.

"We did?" John said.

"We could. Nothing's off the table."

"I think I'm too old for the pain of a tattoo, Mary Margaret." John admitted. "Maybe matching nipple rings. Nothing's off the table, right?" Everyone had a good laugh. Regardless of rekindling relationships with his sons, John felt right at home there, with this mash-up of a family. Blood preferred but not required. He fit right in with no effort at all.

THE END

About the Author

After retiring from Corporate America, she spent her free time volunteering until Covid-19 made those activities obsolete. Not one to sit around and watch *Days of Our Lives*, she decided to write a book. She wrote a couple, so depending on which one hits the shelf first, this could be her debut novel. She is an empty nester of two adult daughters. One husband, a dog, and a cat remain.

Regarding any questions or comments you might have, feel free to reach out at cynthiaakingbooks.com.

www.ingramcontent.com/pod-product-compliance
Lightning Source LLC
Chambersburg PA
CBHW051144120626
46547CB00012B/943